SPLASH!

Increase Your Life's Impact

John Bonesio
Rena Bonesio, MSW

Published in Roseville, California by Simply Great Lives

Library of Congress Control Number: 2014910210

ISBN 978-0-9904039-0-6

First Edition

To our kids, Nathan and David
who give us hope for the future.

Table of Contents

1

Reality Check

No matter how much we try to run away from this thirst for the answer to life, for the meaning of life, the intensity only gets stronger and stronger. We cannot escape these spiritual hungers.

– Ravi Zacharias

Imagine this scenario...

You've been feeling strange for a few days now. You feel aches and pain in your shoulders and upper arms, and you don't know why. The doctor checked it out, but there doesn't seem to be anything wrong.

Now, it's the middle of the night. The pain is so strong it wakes you up. You can't get back to sleep. Suddenly, your heart starts beating really hard for a couple of beats and you feel sick to your stomach. Terrified, you lay curled up on the floor of the bathroom, and wonder if maybe you're dying.

The reality sinks in that this could be the end. You start thinking about your kids; how they will grow up not knowing you. Your spouse will have to raise the kids and go on without you.

You imagine that you won't show up at work on Monday or any day thereafter. Will your coworkers care much? Or will they just get a replacement and move on? You wonder if the world will notice.

You ask yourself some really big, life-sized questions:

"Did I love people well?"

"Did my life matter?"

2

Why You Need to Read This Book

All men dream, but not equally. Those who dream by night in the dusty recesses of their minds, wake in the day to find that it was vanity: but the dreamers of the day are dangerous men, for they may act on their dreams with open eyes, to make them possible.

– T. E. Lawrence

The scenario you just read describes exactly what happened to me (John) when I had a heart attack in 2005. And I was not satisfied with my answers to those two big questions.

I am grateful for my heart attack experience, though, because it forced me to reevaluate my life while I still had time to do things differently. I had a second chance, a second lease on life, and I was determined to make it worthwhile.

I've heard from other people who have faced death that they had a similar experience. I believe everyone will eventually ask themselves important questions evaluating their time spent on earth.

Because of this, I feel compelled to tell people that at some point, they will also be asking themselves if they loved people well and if their lives mattered.

My ultimate hope is that people will consider these questions long before they are at death's door.

It would be a tragedy to look back at the end of life and realize that we didn't spend nearly enough of our time, energy and money on the things we value most, and that our life had no real lasting impression on the world.

If you have reached a point in your life where you resonate with the idea of living a life of greater significance, if "normal" isn't good enough any more, if you're looking for something more, then read on.

This book is based on my and my wife, Rena's, journey. It is based on our journey since that difficult day to discover our purpose and positively impact the lives of other people. It is a journey that continues throughout our lives because we are never really done learning. We certainly don't claim to know everything and we can't anticipate every situation. We are just sharing our experience here in the hope that it can save you some needless time floundering around like we did.

Our Experience

John's Story

I was only 38 years old when I had my heart attack. Sure, I had done some good things in my life up until that point. On taking a closer look, however, I saw that I had actually squandered much of my time and opportunities. I had lived mostly reacting to outside influences, letting things happen to me instead of living with intention and purpose. I either let other people set the agenda for my time and efforts, or I did what I felt like doing in the moment. It was painfully obvious to me that I hadn't set clear goals for my life.

Despite the wake-up call of my heart attack, I initially went back to my job and my old way of life. But in the back of my mind, I knew something had changed. My career felt meaningless, and I wanted something different for my life. But what could I really do to change it? I had spent almost twenty years pursuing my career, and my family depended on my six-figure income.

Rena's Story

I (Rena) remember how stressful it was for us during that time. Of course the actual heart attack incident was hard, but the stress had started way before that.

My life was really out of balance. I wanted to do a good job raising my kids. However, I didn't believe being a stay-at-home mom would give me the kind of recognition I wanted. I desperately wanted people to respect me also for my professional abilities.

I decided to start my own business in network marketing. I thought I could juggle an awesome career and be fully available to my kids at the same time. In an attempt to get the admiration I longed for, I pushed hard to gain a position of status in my career.

It was very time-consuming.

At the same time, John had an online business with a friend. He wanted to have time to work on his business and I wanted to have time to work on mine. We frequently argued about who had to "watch the kids." It hurts my heart to even say that now, but that's where we were at in our lives. Honestly, I believe that the stress in our marriage was one of the factors that contributed to John's heart attack.

Furthermore, I wanted a position of status so badly that I stepped outside my own integrity. I paid to sign up members of my team and I placed product orders under their names to meet production requirements. I cheated to become a sales director. It was crazy. That's just not like me. I don't normally operate that way.

Through some personal development work I did with a life coach, I became aware that I based my self-worth on what I thought other people thought of me.

A few months after John's heart attack, I was staffing a workshop with a good friend of mine. On a break, my friend and I walked down a long hall between the meeting room and the bathroom. I became keenly aware of my thoughts as I tried to size up what people were thinking about me as we passed in the hall.

So I asked my friend, "Do you wonder what people are thinking about you as you walk down the hall?"

She said "Pfft! No!"

I exclaimed, "Really?! You can do that?"

I was stunned as I began to fully understand how much I had built my entire life on what other people thought of me. I had laid it as a foundation and built my life on top of it: everything from my career choices, to how I used my time, to the things I chose to say or not say. It was all based, at least to some degree, on what I thought other people would think of me.

Suddenly I realized I didn't have to keep living my life that way.

It triggered in me a complete meltdown. I had the distinct sensation that my life – with all its different components – was completely falling apart. It was collapsing all around me.

I understood that I had the power to choose how to put the pieces of my life back together again and I felt overwhelmed by the possibilities. I could choose what is really important to me, use it as the foundation and then build my life on top of it.

As a result, within a couple months I let go of my business and worked on rearranging my life's priorities, starting with that of raising our two sons. It took years for me to be completely satisfied with being a stay-at-home mom.

What Happened Next

John's story (cont.)

It took several years for me (John) to make the change I desired after my heart attack. I'd like to say I laid down some clear goals and pursued them step-by-step and achieved steady results. But the truth is that I floundered around a lot. I kept my career job for four more years. Each year I was slowly dying on the inside. I could not ignore the yearnings of my heart.

Rena and I went through a personal finance class: Dave Ramsey's Financial Peace University. This class helped us experience a powerful shift in our marriage. We finally worked through our differences regarding how we used our money. We realized that being financially secure put us in a position to better help others and give to causes we found important. After completing the course, we wanted others to achieve financial freedom and give generously as well.

And then, an opportunity presented itself. My company had layoffs, and I lost my job. I wasn't really disappointed about it. We were debt-free at the time, and the severance package gave us a hefty emergency fund. Rena and I were in agreement that we wanted to invest our time into making a difference in people's lives, and we were financially in a position to try something new.

We decided to go through Dave Ramsey's Counselor Training program and start our own financial coaching business. We knew this opportunity would draw on our strengths, and it was a way for us to help people improve their lives.

After all, we believed that what really mattered in life was the contribution we were making in the lives of other people. And that kind of focus has really satisfied us in the long run. In the past, a new car, new clothes or new gadget would make us happy for a little while. A new career felt fulfilling for a while. But the happiness was always fleeting.

It has been a wonderful journey of discovery, and it has brought us closer together because of our shared vision. Ultimately, when we face death, Rena and I want to be confident that we have, in fact, loved people well and that our lives have made a difference.

Why Wouldn't You Get Started?

During those four years between my heart attack and the layoff, I felt that my career had little meaning. I didn't want to make widgets anymore. I wanted to make a significant contribution to the world and see results that were real, tangible and positive.

But I held myself back with these thoughts:

- "If I step out into something else, I will surely fail."
- "People will not want what I have to offer."
- "Who am I to be influencing people? Doesn't that make me arrogant?"
- "I'm probably not good enough anyway."

These mindsets kept me stuck for four whole years. I stayed comfortable with the familiar, paralyzed to act.

If you have wrestled with these same kinds of thoughts, take heart. You're not alone. I know what it's like to stare at a big overwhelming goal, wondering if you should even bother to take that first step.

That's what this book is for, to get you into a good position to find your purpose, make an impact in the world, and do it really well. We will guide you through seven steps to make that happen. There are exercises at the end of each step to help you put what you learn into practice.

Just to Be Clear

This book is not a "How to Start a Business" book. It doesn't ask you to quit your job, start a business or non-profit, give all your money away, or never have nice things again.

This book doesn't ask you to live a life that is incongruent with your values, dreams and goals. On the contrary, this book will guide you to discover and evaluate your values and passions and change your life to match.

We have found that ultimate satisfaction in living comes when we are satisfied with our answers to the questions: "Do I love people well?" and, "Does my life matter?"

Our hearts' desire is for you to make a "splash" in the world by living your legacy; to have a life that is wonderfully satisfying and rewarding.

This book will help you develop a set of personalized steps, a blueprint, that will allow you to find your own purpose in life and make an impact. We will help you find what makes your heart sing and express that to make the world a better place. If you want to discover your purpose, live your calling and increase your influence, this book is for you.

.

3

Your Splash, a Sneak Peek

I don't believe people are looking for the meaning of life as much as they are looking for the experience of being alive.

– Joseph Campbell

You might be wondering what it will look like for you to find your purpose and make a real impact in the world. Just thinking about it can be both scary and exciting at the same time. Let us assure you it's going to be awesome!

First, let's talk about finding your purpose, and living your calling. Your purpose is your own unique combination of strengths and passions used to impact other people's lives. Your purpose is unique to you, an outer expression of your inner qualities and values.

Your strengths, simply put, are the things you love to do and are really good at doing. Your passions, what you get really fired up about, come from your life experiences; they cry out to you to take action in the world. Your strengths and passions can be mixed and matched, which creates a wide variety of options for you to choose from to make an impact. Whichever combination of strengths and passions you choose to use, it will be a powerful expression of who you are.

When you get clear on your purpose, it will make perfect sense to you because it will be just the right match for who you are. You will touch other people's lives in a significant way. And you will be really, really good at it!

By it's nature, your purpose will be other-focused. Your purpose is not about having certain experiences, going places or doing things for your own benefit. We're not talking about a "bucket list."

We're not talking about doing a few random acts of kindness, either. Even well intentioned activities don't always bring the desired results. Instead of focusing on what to do, your purpose will focus on an end result: a positive impact on the lives of other people so their lives are better than they were before.

Living your purpose will require you to be clearly directed, intentional, and focused. You will be personally invested and deeply concerned about the outcome. And as a result of living out your purpose, people's lives will be impacted in the following ways: positive, focused, recognizable, and long-lasting. Let's explore these kinds of impact in more detail.

Positive

The effect you'll have on other people's lives will be extraordinarily positive. Some people, like con artists, child abusers, and terrorists, have a profoundly negative effect on other people. But most people have an overall neutral impact on the lives of other people. There are no lasting signs of their impact on the world.

You are different. You have chosen to be a benefit to other people. It will be obvious that you came into the world and had a powerfully positive impact. That evidence will live on long after you are gone.

Example of Neutral vs. Positive

Donna Chapman had a pretty normal life. She focused mostly on her family, her husband, their adult children and grandchildren. One day, she was at work in a dress shop when her husband and son arrived with some shocking news: her daughter, Tammy, had just been murdered at a gas station when she stopped to fill up on her way to church.

Upon hearing the news, Donna went completely numb; it was too terrible to believe.

After that, Donna met with her deceased daughter's closest friends. She got to know Tammy at a deeper level than ever before. She also attended grief support groups. Over time, Donna began to heal. Other things in her life that used to be a big deal lost their meaning, and now she felt an intense need to help others who also suffered a great loss. Today she helps lead the grief care group at her church, where she uses her experience to give hope to people who are hurting.

If Donna had not experienced the loss of her daughter, she may have continued living a life that had little impact on people beyond her family. Instead, that tragic experience served as a catalyst for her to go out and leave her own positive mark on the world.

Focused

Even with the best of intentions, you won't be able to do all the good in the world that you aspire to do. No one can. The results of your efforts, if spread too thin, will be mediocre at best.

A flashlight spreads a little bit of light over a large area. A laser, on the other hand, focuses it's light to such a degree that it can cut through steel. Your efforts will bring phenomenal results because of your laser-like focus.

Example of Unfocused vs. Focused

Christopher Reeve is probably best known for his leading role in the popular film, *Superman*. In addition to being a talented actor, he was a true philanthropist. As he developed his acting career, he donated a lot of time and money to various organizations and causes. He worked for improvements in the arts, human rights, and the environment, to name a few. Many organizations benefited from his involvement, and the broad range of issues with which he helped demonstrated a very kind and giving heart.

Then Christopher Reeve sustained a serious injury as the result of a horse-riding accident. He began to focus his charitable efforts on disability-related issues, especially regarding spinal cord injuries. He helped start the Reeve-Irvine Research Center at UC Irvine's School of Medicine to improve the treatment of spinal cord injuries. Because of his efforts, the American Paralysis Association's revenue went from $2.5 million to $5 million in just three years'. The organization changed its name to the Christopher Reeve Foundation.

The lives of many people with paralysis have been and continue to be touched by Christopher Reeve. We believe that his choice to focus his charitable efforts resulted in more lives touched at a deeper level than what his less focused efforts would have achieved.

Recognizable

As you live out your purpose, your impact will be easy to see. There won't be any need to guess if you really made a difference or not.

Some results will be easier to measure than others. But there will be a clear "before" and "after." That change will be obvious to an onlooker or could be reported by the person whose life you dramatically impacted.

Example of Unclear vs. Recognizable

As a life coach and active volunteer, Jenny Williamson positively touched many lives, and she most likely would have continued to do so in that capacity. Then she became aware of the issue of child sex trafficking[2]. Shocked and horrified, she learned that not only was it a global issue, but it was happening in her own community.

Jenny Williamson founded the nonprofit organization, Courage Worldwide, and started a home for girls rescued from sex trafficking. Before she started the Courage House, the only option the police had to protect these young victims was to arrest them and put them in jail for prostitution. The results of that intervention were "unclear" at best, since most girls were back in the same situation again once released from jail.

Now, girls are benefiting from this residential program that promotes healing and restoration, so they can be free to explore who they are meant to be. The girls rescued from sex trafficking go from bondage to freedom, from being a slave to being a free person. Because of Jenny's organization, the girls in this program are so dramatically different that they stand out as a crystal clear example of "recognizable."

Long-lasting

Another outcome of living with purpose is that you will bring about long-term change in people's lives. Temporary changes alleviate a problem for only a little while. Then the problem returns, and the people are no better off than they were before.

Of course, it is sometimes necessary to provide immediate help that meets basic human needs, such as providing food for people who are hungry. But you won't be satisfied to stop there, because you'll be working for results that last.

Example of Short-lived vs. Long-lasting

Eugene Lang, a successful business owner, went back to the elementary school he attended as a kid,[3] Public School 121 in East Harlem, to address the students there. His plan was to give a motivational speech on how to succeed if you work hard. Just before he went up to give his speech, the principal told him that 75% of the 6th graders would not graduate from high school. Before he addressed the students, he ripped up the notes for his speech, because he realized that those words would not cause the long-term change he wanted for those kids.

Instead of giving his motivational speech that day, Eugene Lang told the kids that if they graduated high school, he would pay for their college. Consequently, 90% of the kids graduated, and 60% pursued higher education afterward! Of the 61 kids, 54 stayed in touch with him. Eugene Lang caused long-term change. In fact, he went on to create the "I Have a Dream Foundation" where he continues to bring about long-term change in people's lives.

What Your Purpose Is Not

A purpose isn't the same as your role, like that of a parent, spouse or employee. It isn't your job or your career. Your purpose transcends the roles you have. You may live out your purpose by what you do within your role, but roles change over time. If you're a parent, you'll eventually become an empty nester. If you are a spouse, you may become a widow someday. If you are an employee, you may end up changing jobs. You may change how you live out your purpose, but the calling still remains.

Tall, Grande or Vente Sized Impact

You have the power to choose how large your influence will be. The following images represent some options you have regarding the size of your impact. The concentric squares represent your world. Your own life is the center square. Each ring represents different spheres of influence, from family to friends, to acquaintances, to people in your community, to people around the world. The smiley faces are the people whose lives you impact. The bigger the impact, the bigger the smiley face.

Option #1: Zip

The first option, "Zip," is the size of our impact when we focus exclusively on ourselves. Our focus is only on things that make us happy in the moment, plans for our own success, and things and experiences we gather for ourselves. We leave "zip," "zilch," or no impact in the world when we're gone.

Realistically, you wouldn't be spending your time reading this book if this was the option you wanted to choose for yourself.

Option #2: Tall

In the second option, "Tall," we focus not only on ourselves, but also on family and our closest friends. We can get some satisfaction from doing good things for the people we love. Most of our attention is on short-term benefits, but at least we're sharing them with other people.

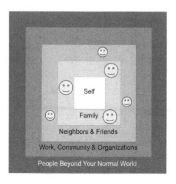

This option is quite popular. Many people feel good about investing their lives in their children and in their grandchildren. Maybe they figure it's someone else's responsibility to make things better in the world.

Option #3: Grande

"Grande," the third option, has us directing more of our focus outward. Not only do our efforts benefit our family and friends, but now they start to impact others in meaningful ways, people we may have hardly gotten to know otherwise. We make deliberate choices in order to make an impact.

Grande's a great way to live life. Our heart's in the right place: we want to make a difference. If we were more deliberate in managing our time, energy and money, we could make an even bigger impact.

Option #4: Vente

The final option, "Vente," is where we are living large! We're efficiently using our life's resources to make deep and significant change that lasts. We are focused. We have found our purpose and are making an impact, and we're doing a great job at it too.

Living this way is truly satisfying. People who choose this option are always learning and improving themselves so they can be more of a benefit to the world.

What's Your Cup of Tea?

We have different "flavors" of Vente-sized impact to choose from as well. One flavor focuses our efforts on people far from us who wouldn't otherwise be a part of our lives.

An advantage to this choice is that it allows us to impact many, many people.

Another flavor of impact focuses our effort on people who are close to us. Building more intimate and trusting relationships can give us an exceptional opportunity to change people at a deeper level. Mentoring and counseling are good examples of touching people's lives at this deep level.

Most likely, the people who benefit from this kind of effort will go on to discover their own purpose and make their own impact in the world.

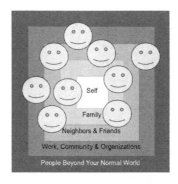

Naturally, we hope everyone goes for the "Vente" option. We believe it will satisfy an innate need to contribute to humanity and make a difference.

Ultimately, having a positive impact on other people is the criterion you will use to evaluate your life. Have you ever been with someone as they approached their final days? Perhaps you got to glimpse a review of their life.

Knowing the end of their life is near, people often show an understanding of the value of others and the importance of relationships. It's not often that people will say, "I really wish I went on that European tour." Instead, they express regret that they didn't spend more time with a loved one, or that they didn't tell that person how much they loved them.

Sometimes, people who have had a brush with death will report seeing their lives flash before their eyes. In our own experience, when John realized he might be dying, he found himself asking, "Did I love people well?" and "Did my life matter?"

Our desire is for you to ask these questions now, long before that time, so you can use the rest of your time on earth to have a positive impact on other people.

The Great

> There is really no such thing as elir......acing a habit. You must replace
> the bad habit with a good one.
>
> – Zig Ziglar

Early on in our marriage, we volunteered leading youth and young adult ministries at our church. After a few years, we had children and turned our focus to our kids. We defaulted to what we saw everyone else doing, focusing on the good life and having nice things for the family. We entered the "bigger-better" hunt, upgrading our house and car when we could, getting the big screen TV, and trying to live an affluent life-style. We didn't think of ourselves as selfish. We were just living the American dream.

None of these individual desires were bad, but they disconnected us from our deepest values. There was no focus. We spent nearly all of our money each month. We were involved in too many things at once. We often didn't have much time left over to spend with others. We were emotionally drained.

Now we have focus. We focus our time, energy, and money on sharing our story – telling people to find their calling and live with impact. We are involved in speaking into people's lives, which is in alignment with our values and heart's desires.

ing from "life as usual" to finding our calling
nge. We traded our ordinary life for one of
e out of focus for one in focus; a life of randomness
meaning. One of the hardest things about this journey is
e trade sometimes involves giving up things we like – even
ngs we spent a lot of effort to obtain.

Often we are told that we can have it all. You may have seen the object lesson of filling a jar full of rocks. The illustration suggests that if we first put the big rocks (the important things) into the jar (our life), then all the little rocks (the less important things) will fit too. But we've found that it likely won't all fit. And there may be some things in life that are not only taking up "space" but are actually in the way. These things are preventing us from achieving a life of significance – from discovering and pursuing our calling.

The good news is that we get to replace these things that we give up for even better things. The book by Jim Collins, *Good to Great*[4], states that 'good' is the enemy of 'great'. The reason is that good seems good enough. We settle and give up on trying for great. There are going to be good things in our life that we will have to give up so we can replace them with great things.

Mindsets

Throughout this book, we will introduce different mindsets. A mindset is a belief, or way of thinking, about how the world works. Sometimes our mindsets are faulty and limit possibilities in our lives. New ways of thinking are needed to break free of old patterns. Our thinking can be the biggest barrier to getting what we want, or pursuing what we feel is truly important.

Each mindset is an exchange in which we trade the old thought pattern for the new pattern. We will introduce each old mindset, and then turn it into the positive pattern we need to establish in its place.

The World Is Waiting for Us

Feelings of unworthiness can run deep and will show up in negative self-talk like: "Who am I to be doing this?" or "I'm not good enough, rich enough, or important enough to be doing this."

Feelings of unworthiness run deeper than just feeling incompetent. If we don't have the skills to do something, at some level in our subconscious we usually believe we could if we acquired the skills. But when we feel unworthy, it's an issue of a negative self-view. Instead of the problem being a lack of skills, which we can acquire, it's a limiting view of who we are at our core.

We want you to know that if you withdraw from the challenge, if you shrink back and play life small, the world is missing out! There is no one else just like you, and the world will not get to experience the full you if you don't show up.

The world needs you to contribute. Everybody has his or her own unique strengths and passions. God has wired you up uniquely. You were created for a purpose, and that purpose is your calling.

When we fully understand this, our worthiness doesn't even enter into the picture. We aren't focused on our own worthiness. Instead, we focus on our contribution to the world, and on how we can be a benefit to others.

The only way to shed feelings of unworthiness is by taking one step at a time toward your calling. Read this book, and do the exercises at the end of each chapter. As you take one step and then another, and then another, you will start to believe that you are the kind of person who pursues a calling.

The world is waiting for you.

Dreams vs. Fortune

Advertising and magazine covers give us the message that we should pursue our fortune. We should work to make a good income so we can live a nice lifestyle and have nice things. This book gives the opposite message, that of taking the other path and pursuing our passions first.

Some folks will suggest that we can acquire even more money by following our dreams and passions. This may be true, but it muddies the discussion because the focus continues to be about pursuing one's fortune. This isn't the point. The point is that if we pursue our passions and dreams, we will be satisfied and content, and as long as our needs are met, the money really won't matter as much to us.

The key here is to primarily pursue the things that will bring us ultimate satisfaction in life rather than pursue the things that only bring us temporary gratification. We're not saying that having nice things is wrong or that we should avoid these things. It's just that acquiring money and things will not satisfy our inner longings. When we pursue and live our calling, we are satisfied. In this emotional space, money moves to its proper place as just one tool that we use to express our deepest values in the world.

The 7 Steps

We've examined our own journey of personal development, and identified seven important steps in this process. We wrestled through the steps very carefully to come up with the sequence. The order of the steps is important as they build on one another. Each person's journey through the steps will look different depending on their situation and needs, but the order of the steps should still be the same.

The seven steps are:

1. Make Time
2. Connect to Positive Inputs
3. Maximize Your Energy
4. Build Security at Home
5. Discover Your Purpose
6. Learn by Experience
7. Live Your Calling and Refine

Each step involves an exchange, replacing an old behavior or life pattern with a new one that will move you forward. Here is an overview of the seven steps.

Step 1: Make Time
Replace unfocused time with focused time

Most of us are way too busy. We can't fit all our activities in by just doing the important things first. We are going to have to remove some things from our life so that we can devote time to finding and pursuing our calling.

Step 2: Connect to Positive Inputs
Replace negative influences with positive influences

There are always outside influences ready to get us down. They may be in the form of our friends and family, or they may be messages from our own negative self-talk. Perhaps the news we pay attention to can bring us down. The key to success relies on reducing our exposure to these negative influences and increasing our exposure to encouraging, supportive, positive influences.

We're not looking for "yes" people that only say what we want to hear. We're looking for truth delivered to us in a way that moves us forward rather than messages that keep us stuck.

Step 3: Maximize Your Energy

Replace a draining environment with a filling environment

There may be things in our environment that drag on us mentally. We can't stop thinking about them. Or they drain us emotionally. If that job we go to every day frequently makes us want to cry, we will not likely have the emotional energy to contribute to others. This step is about reducing or removing environmental factors that affect the amount of energy we have to devote to our calling.

Step 4: Build Security at Home

Replace shaky ground with sure footing

The concept behind this step is that when we are feeling secure at home, we are able to tolerate greater risks in other areas of our life. To pursue our calling, we may need to attempt new things that require personal risk. We may feel called, for example, to take some financial risk to help others. If we are in debt, living paycheck to paycheck, or if we don't feel safe, we will feel stuck. This step is about freeing ourselves up to take necessary, appropriate risks to move forward.

Step 5: Discover Your Purpose

Replace doing what feels good at the time with following a purpose and a plan

This step is about discovering our big "why" in life. We don't want our lives to be random. We need to keep focused on things we care deeply about. There are numerous great things to which we can contribute or even start.

One of the big hurdles we often face, though, is burnout. Burnout can result when we help in a way that doesn't use our strengths or when we contribute to a cause to which we weren't called. In this step, we explore our strengths and passions. Then we clarify our direction in life with a written purpose statement. The purpose statement is a tool that will help to point us in the right direction toward our calling.

Step 6: Learn By Experience
Replace head knowledge with experience

We can get a good idea of our purpose through self-reflection and thinking, but we can't really know for certain what our purpose is until we've put it into action. We need to "try it on for size" and "take it for a spin around the block". Our experience may confirm our purpose, or it may prompt us to go back and revise our purpose statement. Either way, the experience we gain in this step can provide clarity about what we should do for our calling.

Step 7: Live Your Calling and Refine
Replace a smaller impact with a larger impact

Once we have determined our calling, it's time to increase the size of our impact, our "splash," in the world. We can't assume that activity equals results. This step is about refining our efforts to produce more meaningful change with longer lasting effects.

Exercises

The next set of chapters will dig deeper into each step. At the end of each chapter there will be exercises for you to do. The temptation will be to read straight through the book. However, you will get the most out of this book if you do the exercises as you read. If you do just read the book through, please come back later to the exercises, as they will help you on your journey.

Stories of the Called

Later in this book, you will find chapters that tell the stories of ordinary people who have discovered their calling. A calling rarely, if ever, just falls into our laps. There is usually a process of discovery, and then we experience a process of stepping into our calling. The stories of these individuals will show what this process can look like, what obstacles they faced, and how they broke through into their calling.

Many of these folks we interviewed experienced some connection to God as a part of their discovery process. Some wrestled with God. Some felt they received confirmation about their calling from God. Some didn't feel any connection to God in the process at all. Just to be clear, a connection to, or faith in God is not a requirement to discover and pursue our calling.

During the interviews, we asked these folks questions about their discovery process; the obstacles, the breakthroughs, and their experience of life now that they are living their calling. We also asked them what advice they would give to someone looking to discover his or her own calling. We hope that one, if not all, of these stories will resonate with your own experience.

Now, let's dive into the seven steps.

5

Step 1: Make Time

Replace unfocused use of time with focused use of time

Lost time can never be found.

– Benjamin Franklin

When we first decided to start our financial coaching business on the side, our plan was to develop it on weekends and evenings. However just as we were diving in, I (John) was let go from my daytime career. I could have continued to look for work, but we decided it was time to venture out on our own.

Not having a 40+ hour workweek was fantastic. With more time available, we could be more creative, better evaluate our progress, and focus our attention.

Of course, not everyone has the opportunity to walk away from a regular full-time job. Needs and options vary from person to person. The important thing to understand for this step is that if life is too full, it is simply too challenging to devote the necessary time, energy, and money to pursue one's calling.

How Much Time?

In my younger years, I had an idea that someday I would get around to finding my purpose in life. I spent a little time brainstorming, reading a book now and then. I even created a personal mission statement - several of them, in fact. But when it came down to it, I just didn't devote enough time to it.

If finding and living our calling is a back burner project, we won't really do what we need to do to get it done. It requires time and action. Our first step, Make Time, is the most specific step of all the seven steps. For Step 1, we need to free up at least 10 hours a week to devote to our calling.

Why 10 hours? Well, there's some leniency to the actual time amount, but let us explain why we chose 10 hours.

If we had only 2 hours a week to do this work, we might try to get it done in the in-between times of busy life. Not much progress could be made on realizing our true calling. We'd be cramming, just like we did in school, trying to finish up projects and study for tests. We'd be trying to complete the steps under a time pressure. If we're cramming, we aren't able to put as much creativity into the process. There is a great study that explains why.

The Candle Problem

Author Dan Pink, who wrote a book titled *Drive*, gave a TED Talk presentation (http://www.ted.com). He shared in one of his presentations about a social experiment where researchers introduced what they called "the candle problem" to their research subjects. Participants stood at a cubicle desk and were given a candle, a book of matches and a box of thumbtacks. They were told to fix the candle to the wall so that it didn't drip on the table when lit.

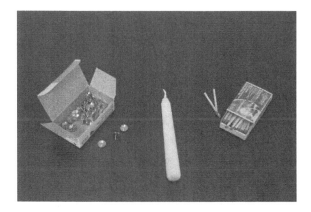

The first idea that most people had was to melt the candle wax and try to stick the candle to the wall, but that doesn't work. The actual solution that people were supposed to discover required using the box that held the thumbtacks.

The researchers started with a control group. The control group was told to just solve the problem. The researchers then recorded how long it took the group on average to solve the problem.

Then they tested a second group. They told this group that they were going to be tested to see how fast they could solve the problem. They were also given an incentive that if they were in the fastest 25%, they'd get five dollars. If they were the fastest person to solve the problem, they'd get twenty dollars.

Which group do you think performed the fastest? It was the first group, the one with no time expectations. The second group took on average three and half minutes longer to solve the problem. Yep, you read that right. The group that was trying to be the fastest and that had incentives for a quick solution actually took longer!

This experiment shows that when we are under time pressure, our thinking narrows. We get more focused. The trouble is that narrow, focused thinking diminishes creativity.

Pursuing our calling is a highly creative process. If we attempt to work through these steps in the in-between spaces (e.g., when we're driving or going from one appointment to the next), we're under considerable time pressure. We hinder our creativity.

You might not end up needing the full 10 hours each week, but if you plan for that time at the beginning of the week, you are free to engage in full creative thinking. You can always adjust the time later in the week if, for example, you've accomplished a goal and want to celebrate.

Keep in mind that when you finally get to the place where you are actively living your calling, 10 hours is going to seem way too short.

Too Busy?

Most of us feel too busy. We have our kids' activities, PTA meetings, church groups, overtime hours at work, weekend chores and honey-do lists. It seems like every time we turn around, the car needs to be fixed, we need haircuts or new clothes, we have doctor appointments, and there are birthday and holiday parties to attend. Let's face it, we have a lot going on in our lives.

At this point, you're probably wondering, "How in the world am I going to fit in one more thing?" Truthfully, you probably can't.

Don't worry, because there are options. But before we explore those options, we need to look at some mindsets that will either help us or hinder us when it comes to time.

Mindsets

When we brought up the goal of 10 hours a week, our guess is that you might have had a conversation with yourself that went something like this:

Me #1: "OK, I know this will take work. Anything worth doing takes effort, right? Let's do this!"

Me #2: "Yeah, right. There's no way you have time to make this happen. You have to go to Bobby's soccer games and football games, and get Sally to her piano lessons. Just when you get started, you know your boss is going to ask for overtime work. Get real."

Isn't it fun to argue with yourself? It certainly makes for great material to use in a comedy routine, but in reality, if we're not internally "of one mind", we're going to resist going forward. So, let's talk about some negative thought patterns that might prevent us from going forward with this first step of making time.

We are in the Driver's Seat

In order to be able to devote some time to our calling, we first need to get control over our day's activities. One of the most common, unproductive thought patterns we see is thinking that we're not in control. We use language like, "I have to ..." or "I can't..." as if we don't have any choices. The truth is that we always have choices - lots of them.

Yet many of us go through life just reacting to external circumstances. We feel forced to go down a certain path, like life is happening to us. This is known as victim mentality.

The benefit of victim mentality is that we don't have to be responsible for anything. We can always blame someone or something else. We may think and say things like: it's that other driver's fault; my boss is making my life miserable; I'm late to work because of traffic; the Great Recession made me lose my house.

This kind of thinking costs us dearly, though. First, it takes us out of the driver's seat of our life. We are always at the mercy of someone or something else. Second, we're powerless to fix anything. For example, if our problems at work are our boss's fault, we are stuck waiting for him or her to fix the problem. We've relinquished responsibility and put our boss in the driver's seat of our life.

There is a quote from the musician, John Lennon, which illustrates this type of victim mentality:

> *"Life is what happens when you're making other plans."*

I guess even successful folks can still get caught up in victim mentality.

Is it any wonder that this type of thinking affects how we spend our time? When we engage in victim mentality, we aren't in control over our own time. We are at the mercy of circumstances and other people.

Let's talk about the alternative. We'll call this "empowerment mentality."

Mindset 1: Empowerment Mentality

Old thinking: "I have to.../I can't..."

New thinking: "I choose to..."

When we don't take responsibility for the choices we make, we forfeit the power to choose something different for ourselves. Therefore, there is a lot of power in recognizing our part in what we might otherwise consider to be our "circumstances." We need to recognize our own power to make changes in our lives before we will have the power to affect changes in the lives of other people.

This alternative is to see that we have contributed to the situation. Now, this is different from blaming oneself. It is just seeing that we have made choices. And instead of trying to assign a value to these choices, right or wrong, good or bad, let's just look at them as neutral.

When we stop using victim thinking, we use a different phrase. We say, "I choose to..." because we have control over our life. Perhaps we don't control everything, but we do control some things - a lot of things. We would say things like: "I choose to remain at work where I don't get along with my boss; I chose to leave for work at the last minute which left no time if there was traffic; I chose to stop paying on my mortgage and didn't look for other options, so the bank foreclosed on me."

Again, this is not about assigning blame. Don't play the blame-shame game, not even with yourself. It's not productive. It doesn't matter whose fault it is. What matters is that we made some choices and now we get to make some new choices.

A comparison between victim mentality and empowerment mentality is illustrated in a recent quote from John Maxwell in an interview with Michael Hyatt[5]:

> *"Most people don't lead their lives. Instead, they just accept their lives."*

When we use empowerment mentality, we are back in control over our lives. If we've been making choices that we don't like, we now get to make some different choices. We get to lead our life rather than just accept it.

Here's a simple way to tell which type of mentality we're using. If we are affected to a large degree by circumstances and others, we are probably using victim mentality. If others and circumstances are affected by us, we are probably using empowerment mentality.

Empowerment mentality allows us to make time to pursue our calling. We choose how we spend our time, and we can choose to spend some of it on priorities that benefit us in the long run.

Options

We limit our options unnecessarily when we believe there are only two choices available to us: option A or option B. We think things like:

- "If cable TV isn't available to me, then I have to get satellite TV."
- "If I don't get that job at We Make Stuff Inc., then there aren't any jobs and I'm stuck in unemployment."
- "I have to buy that house for sale near my workplace, or I'll be stuck with a long commute."

A or B Thinking can easily lead to victim mentality. When one of the options becomes unavailable, we believe we are forced into the other option.

We might reveal A or B thinking when we ask for advice on a decision we're making. We'll tell our buddy, "Help me with this decision. I can do option A, but on the other hand I can do option B." Usually both options have drawbacks to them, which is why we're having a hard time making the decision. Option A has some good things, but also some bad things, and Option B has a different set of good and bad things. So we make the choice that seems less bad. Not very exciting, is it?

The truth is that life doesn't give us just two choices at every decision point. There are

> ### Mindset 2: Abundant Options
>
> Old thinking: "I have two options, A or B."
>
> New thinking: "I have many options."
>
> We are fooling ourselves when we believe there are only two choices or, worse, when we believe there are no choices at all. A or B thinking is just a different version of victim mentality. We will have more power over our own lives when we search for a variety of options before we make our decision. The truth is there is an abundance of options available. Brainstorming solutions will reveal new options, usually with at least one of them being better than the first two we started with.

actually an abundance of options. Instead of just A and B, there are also options C, D, E, F, G, H, ... We call this mindset "Abundant

Options." If we take the time to lay out our options, we often find one that is better than the first two we were considering.

Let's take one of the examples from the list above: "I have to buy that house for sale near my workplace, or I'll be stuck with a long commute." What could be some other options?

1. Buying a different house near one's workplace instead of that particular one.
2. Getting a new job closer to home.
3. Renting a home near work and either selling one's current home or renting it out.
4. Looking into better commute options such as carpooling, ride sharing or public transportation.
5. Looking for other work positions in a different location (change jobs and houses together).
6. Telecommuting in one's current position.
7. Starting a small business locally, which over time may enable quitting the current job.

Now there are nine options open to think about (these seven options plus the original two). Maybe after looking at these options, one would decide that relocating to a brand new job is the most appealing choice.

Time Management

With the empowerment and abundant choices mentalities available to us, we're ready to open up options about how we spend our time. Let's talk about what can be shifted to make 10 hours per week available to pursue our calling.

A lot of time management books make the assumption that somehow we can fit it all in and get it all done. But in reality, we can have so much activity in our lives that we're bursting at the seams, so to speak. For many of us, we're going to have to "steal" time from something else so we can devote it to our calling.

For most people, just adding ten hours of activity to the week isn't going to work. Unfortunately, no matter how many science documentaries we watch with our kids, we haven't found a way to use Einstein's Theory of Relativity and time travel to add an additional ten hours to our week, though our twelve year old is convinced he will figure this out any day now. All kidding aside, we believe it's possible to make ten hours available.

To be clear, we don't want you to have to get rid of all your down time. The goal is to find those ten hours you can devote to your calling. Following are a few areas where you might find some time you can repurpose.

Reduce Screen Time

We Americans spend a lot of hours in front of various screens each week. Whether its a TV, computer or smart phone, it can gobble up a lot of the time we could be using for our calling. Some of that screen time we can eliminate, some we can reduce.

TV

We all love stories, and TV helps us get our story fix. Unfortunately, TV programming is designed to make it easy to keep watching and it's really easy to get caught up and watch more than we intended.

According to a 2012 Nielsen report, Americans spend, on average, 34 hours each week in front of the TV[6]. Thirty-four hours is just an average, which means that some folks are spending way more. Whoa! That's a lot of TV watching.

If we want to devote 10 hours a week to pursuing our calling, watching less TV is probably the simplest solution. An added benefit to cutting back on TV is that we reduce the amount of advertising we are exposed to. When we cut out our cable service, we noticed that our level of "I wants" went way down and we were more content with our lives.

Internet and Social Media

A 2012 survey from eMarketer showed that people on average are spending 173 minutes per day on the Internet (almost 3 hours)[7]. Another Nielsen survey showed that people spend most of their time online (22.5%) using social media and blogs[8].

If we spend an hour or two (or more) per day online, it would be relatively easy to repurpose that time for pursuing our calling.

The Internet can be a really useful tool in our lives. It's a lot like TV, though, in that it's easy to spend more time on it than we meant to. So let's be mindful of where the time goes and how we're using it.

One option is to be more focused in how we use our online time. For example, we could allot 15-30 minutes per day to check in on Facebook, Twitter, Pinterest, etc. Then we could have a day of the week where we catch up on all the blogs we're following. Having focused online time might be enough to free up those 10 hours.

Adjust Commitments

Some of us are overcommitted. Maybe we signed up for the PTA, we coach the soccer team, we have 2 weekly groups we attend, we are the organizer for our church's charity ministry, and we are running the school's canned food drive fundraiser.

With this type of schedule, there's really no effective way to pursue our calling. So, we'll have to give something up. The hard part is that all of our activities look like priorities and it's hard to let any of them go.

As we move through the process of discovering our purpose and living our calling, we'll be getting clearer on what types of activities fit in with our calling. Until then, we can consider letting go of things like "warm body commitments." A warm body commitment doesn't require any special skill or ability that we uniquely provide. It can be filled by anybody, so we should let someone else do that work for now.

For some of us, dropping a single commitment can free up quite a few hours per week. It will also remove a heavy load on our life, freeing up mental capacity to pursue our calling.

Maximize Commute Time

With the cost of living rising in the major metropolitan areas, people are commuting longer and longer to work, with more and more traffic. If we spend even 30 minutes each way commuting, we are spending five hours each week just traveling. There are some creative ways to either do some stuff for our calling during our commute or to take care of some things in order to free up some other time we can use for our calling later

Traveling by train, plane or any other mode of transportation where someone else is getting us where we need to go may allow us to do things like:

- Make phone calls
- Write (journaling, emails and other correspondence, blogging)
- Read books that support us in pursuing our calling

If we're doing the driving ourselves, we can still do things like:

- Listen to audio books and podcasts related to our calling
- Voice record notes about things to follow up on. (Using a clip-on microphone makes it easier to do hands-free voice recording)
- connect with friends and mentors by phone

I (John) do a lot of traveling for my work. I really try to be diligent about using my time well. I'm pretty good about it, but, just like anyone else, sometimes I forget to bring an audio book in my car, I get on the plane and zone out, or I get caught up in a movie in the hotel. While we won't be perfect at it, we can still get a lot of useful time for our calling from our commute. Be aware, though, it usually requires some advance planning to be able to make the most of our commute time.

Use Time Blocking

If none of the previous options are working, there is another way to free up time.

Earlier in the book, we mentioned the object lesson with the jar of rocks. While we disagreed that everything will always fit, this object lesson is still right on when it comes to fitting in the big rocks (the important things) first. Then we can try to fit in the little rocks (the less important things). At least this way, if we have to leave some things out of our lives, we leave out the less important ones.

We can make sure we fit the important priorities into our schedule by using a technique called "time blocking." Time blocking is a calendar tool where we write our important activities into blocks of time. We treat these blocks of time like we have an appointment with ourselves and then follow through.

To get 10 hours a week to devote to our calling, we would block out, for example, two specific hours on Sundays and two specific hours every Monday through Thursday. We have an appointment with ourselves for those hours, and we don't schedule anything else during those blocks of time.

If we do need to schedule something over one of our time blocks, we need to reschedule that time block just like we would if we had a schedule conflict with anyone else.

Following is an example of a schedule with time blocks filled into it:

GMT-08	Sun 11/25	Mon 11/26	Tue 11/27	Wed 11/28	Thu 11/29	Fri 11/30	Sat 12/1
8am							
9am		8:30 – 5:30p Work	8:30 – 5:30p Work	8:30 – 5:30p Work	8:30 – 5:30p Work	8:30 – 5:30p Work	8:30 – 10:30 Billy's Soccer Game
10am							
11am							
12pm							
1pm	1p – 4p Family Time						
2pm							
3pm							
4pm							
5pm	5p – 7p Appointment: My Calling						
6pm							
7pm		7p – 9p Appointment: My Calling	7p – 9p Appointment: My Calling	7p – 9p Appointment: My Calling	7p – 9p Appointment: My Calling		
8pm							
9pm							

Whenever we schedule in a time block, we are putting a big rock into our jar. Then the less important things will just need to fit in around it, or not fit in at all.

It's a good idea to put other 'big rock' items on our calendar as well. This way we can see how much unscheduled time we really have for those 'small rock' activities.

Key Points

- Life can get too busy. We need to make room in our schedule to discover and pursue our calling.

- We need to give ourselves sufficient time (around 10 hours a week), so we are able to think creatively.

- We can make time available by making better use of our existing time, or by removing activities that aren't as important.

Exercises

1. Decide which TV shows, if any, you're going to stop watching and put the list in writing.

2. Make a plan for your Internet usage. How frequently are you going to be on the Internet or on social media? What times during the day?

3. List ways you can reclaim some of your commute time. Make a plan to put a couple of them into practice.

4. Add time blocks for pursuing your calling into your calendar.

6

Brian Sharp

Business Developer

If your actions inspire others to dream more, learn more, do more and become more, you are a leader.

– John Quincy Adams

Brian Sharp has been an entrepreneur since he was a boy. It just seemed natural to him. He grew up around other families who owned businesses, and his dad always owned one as well.

As a kid, Brian worked paper routes, did cleaning and yard services, and was a DJ for his junior high school dances. He discovered that he really liked having the ability to create his own income. Buying his own skateboards and water skis was a very empowering experience for him.

In high school, while a lot of his friends were working minimum wage jobs, Brian worked in commissioned jobs making a nice income. He had a realization back then: "the more you take control and the more responsibility you assume, the better things can be." Now Brian can't imagine life being any other way. He is just wired up to build businesses.

Like most entrepreneurs, Brian loves the freedom that comes from owning his own business. He likes being able to say "when, and where, and how and why." The very best part for Brian, though, is being able to make a difference in the lives of other people, starting first with his own family. He explains, "We're blessed because my wife has never had to work since we had children. That was a goal I wrote down when I was 18 years old. I also wanted to be home enough to raise my family. My dad, as an entrepreneur, was not able to do that."

Today, Brian is living his calling by spurring other business owners to success. He accomplishes this through several different means. Over the last several years, he has consulted with and coached business owners. Having built many successful businesses, he is well qualified to give that kind of advice.

Brian spends the bulk of his effort on developing businesses. He starts, builds, and then sells successful companies. It's a great scenario: Brian gets to do the work he loves, and someone else gets a business that is already up and running, and doing well. He explains, "I really enjoy building businesses, and then helping others take the reigns so they can do something they've always wanted to do."

Brian's insurance agency is a good example. He owned the business for six or seven years when he left to start another company. He had been grooming somebody to take over the agency. He recalls, "One of the proudest days I've had was the day I told her that she was ready to own it. She didn't know how that was going to happen, or when, or where, or why. And I remember her becoming very emotional because it was a dream of hers, but she just didn't know how to get there." As an entrepreneur, Brian is able to reach back and pull other people across the gap to where he is.

Brian is also very passionate about motivational speaking. He loves motivating business owners to success by sharing his story and useful information. Most recently, Brian has been building an online business called Presenter Box. It allows business owners to share their messages through video to customers and potential customers. This endeavor has been particularly exciting for Brian, because it blends his love of public speaking, helping business owners to succeed, and building a new business from the ground up.

Brian explains that there are moments when a business owner needs affirmation to really know he or she is succeeding. One of these times for Brian was when he got super busy doing his business-building work. He recalls, "Sometimes when you pursue your calling as an entrepreneur, you put your head down and blinders on. Your business is all you do; it's all you think about. You eat, sleep, drink, and bleed it, and you forget the progress you're making."

During one of those times, Brian had a meeting with his advisor. Brian describes what happened, "He looked at me very flippantly because I was probably complaining about something. He said, 'Do you realize, you're probably a millionaire by now?'"

When Brian checked, he discovered it was true. It was the furthest thing from his mind though, because he was so busy doing work that was really fun for him.

Another affirmation came not long ago from a highly successful friend who works for a high tech company in Silicon Valley. The friend said to Brian, "You know, I've always admired your ability and willingness to take risks." The funny thing was that Brian had been admiring this friend because he had gone the traditional route: he went to college, got a great job, and moved up through the ranks. His friend had been recruited to great companies and earned a lot of money. Yet they shared a mutual admiration for each other. Brian realized, "Oh, okay, I guess I am doing something."

Brian talks about some of the general challenges entrepreneurs face. "It's really kind of a twisted path as an entrepreneur. Sometimes it takes five years before you realize you are one, and you're actually going to pull it off. Most people around you doubt you. Sometimes their support system doubts them. Sometimes you begin to doubt yourself."

Brian explains that our society's beliefs can be a real obstacle to living one's calling. While some schools are starting to teach principles like Steven Covey's *Seven Habits of Highly Effective People*, our society has a long way to go before seeing the pursuit of one's calling as the norm.

When asked about the obstacles he has personally had to confront, Brian replied, "When? Today? This morning? Or yesterday? They're every day." He has faced some really big ones. The first one came in his early twenties, when he had just realized that his insurance agency was going to succeed. He had loaned a car to a friend who got in a terrible accident. As a result, Brian was sued. He lost everything. In fact, he ended up living in his office because he was homeless.

After working through the process of losing everything and rebuilding again, Brian and his wife had a bad medical scare with their son. Brian describes what happened. "While I was in the hospital, someone was embezzling from our largest company. You know, the six-figure kind. As a matter of fact, it was my best friend." The bookkeeper wasn't paying payroll taxes, either. There was a whole lot going wrong at the same time.

Brian says, "I think that anybody who pursues their calling will face a series of challenges, one after the other. It's a test, helping you to decide if you're really in, and if you want it that bad."

Brian tells people who want to live their calling, "You've got to find someone who's already doing it well, and who's doing it in alignment with your values and your goals. That's really where the magic happens, because you can run together. Then you can work with and for them and find a way to glean information and experience from that person. It's like being in a great internship.

Regarding living one's calling, Brian often tells people, "Be proactive, be bold and be patient." He says, "Your calling is not going to fall on your head and say, 'Hey, dude!'" At least, that's not how it works for most people." He continues, "You've got to be proactive and do something. You've got to be bold. You've got to be willing to be told 'no' and that 'you're crazy.' You've got to be willing to take a risk." He says these things are just a part of finding your calling.

"I think that anybody who pursues their calling will face a series of challenges, one after the other. It's a test, helping you to decide if you're really in, and if you want it that bad."

Lastly, Brian says that you've got to be patient. The honeymoon can be over quickly sometimes when you follow your calling. It's not usually easy. It's not what you think it's going to be, like on TV. It takes time.

It breaks Brian's heart to hear people say, "I want to..." or "I've always thought about..." yet they aren't taking action toward those goals. "It bums me out that there are people who don't get to feel that rush, the craziness, the boldness, or that hunger. Their mind isn't always racing and thinking about the next big thing that they want to do."

Brian loves that the excitement of living this way is an integral part of his family's life. He says, "My wife has a calling and she's just a student of it. It's so cool that in our house, our kids are around two people who are in pursuit of something. We're not just settling. We're not just coming home and making dinner and watching TV and going to bed. That's not enough for us."

Brian concludes, "So I think that if you're reading this book, and you think you've got a calling...go for it! But you know what? Take some people with you, because there are other people who need to see you pursuing that, people who are too afraid to start. I think that is just as important as anything else you do."

7

Step 2: Connect to Positive Inputs

Replace negative influences with positive influences

"Be careful the environment you choose for it will shape you; be careful the friends you choose for you will become like them."

– W. Clement Stone

I remember when I (Rena) stopped watching the evening news. At the time, our first son was just an infant, and every night there were stories showing atrocities committed against children: a parent who accidentally ran the car over her toddler; children being sexually abused at a daycare; a child dying of heat exposure when the caregiver left him in the car while shopping. The horrifying stories rolled in, night after night. It was getting me down, so I took a stand and shut off the evening news. I made a decision to not let that negativity into my life any more. With a new baby to care for, I needed my thoughts to be on happier things.

Like John said before, we stopped watching regular TV years ago. We made a conscious decision to limit the amount of junk flowing into our home by shutting off the cable. There's no channel surfing. If we are going to watch something, we are very intentional about it. We watch a lot of documentaries. If we watch a TV show, we usually watch one series at a time, from the first episode to the last. We are very picky about the inputs we choose to plug in to.

We make an effort to plug into positive influences. We have become sponges, soaking up as much positive and useful information as we can: podcasts, books, radio shows, blogs, workshops, classes, and trainings. And we have surrounded ourselves with positive and supportive people: a great professional networking group, supportive friends, Bible study groups and church, a business coach, and a health coach. The support system we've built is an essential part of being able to benefit other people. We have an important message to share with the world and we can't afford to let negative people drain us of our positive energy.

What Are Inputs?

For our purposes, an input is any message that affects the way we think, feel, or behave. We think differently in some way after a particular message is 'put in' our minds. The effect can be large or small. It can be immediate or cumulative over time. Sometimes it's hard to recognize the effect. Whatever that change is, though, the change is what makes a message an input.

The messages we receive can affect any of our feelings. They affect our mood, level of confidence, feelings of self-worth, hope, peace, and sense of security. These messages influence our thoughts about what we can expect in the future, our understanding of how things work, and our beliefs about why things happen the way they do. They affect our ideas of what is possible and what is likely. They can color our beliefs about what we and other people are capable of doing.

Our feelings affect our thoughts, and our thoughts affect our feelings. Because inputs change our thoughts and feelings, they in turn have a profound effect on our actions—what we choose to do or not to do. For example, we might believe successful people are successful because they are lucky. This can then lead us to think we could never do anything of great significance, since it's based on luck anyway. Because of the inputs we are connected to, we might be afraid to step out, be courageous, try new things, and take risks that would result in making a significant contribution to humankind. There is scientific evidence that supports this observation.

Programmers and Bugs

In 2010, researchers studied the effect of messages on software programmers and their ability to solve problems.[9] The programmers were given 5 bugs to fix. The messages on the screen given to the programmers by the testing system would be either positive or negative in nature.

The positive messages included phrases like: "You've made progress," "Quality idea!" or "You've improved the program," and ended with various messages like, "Only four bugs remaining." The negative messages, on the other hand, had phrases like: "Execution failure!" or "The program was rejected," and ended with various messages like "Fix this error!"

The first bug was solved by just about everyone. Then with the subsequent bugs, the success rate of the participants with the negative messages started to dramatically drop. On the second bug, just under 60% of the group with negative messages succeeded, as opposed to over 65% of the group with positive messages. This trend continued until the last bug, where less than 40% of the group with negative messages succeeded at the task. This means that over 60% of the group with negative messages gave up. The group with positive messages maintained a success rate at just over 65%.

The messages we receive in life matter. They affect our ability to solve problems, which has far reaching ramifications throughout our life. Many of life's activities require creativity and problem solving, from job hunting, to resolving conflicts in relationships, to discovering our calling, to name a few.

So let's examine the various inputs we receive in our life and see if we can tip the balance from more negative messages to mostly positive messages.

People as Inputs

By their nature, messages ultimately come from other people. We get a lot of inputs directly from the people in our lives, like family, friends, neighbors, coworkers, service providers and others in the community. Pastors, teachers, elected officials, doctors, and experts are often "inputs" because they tend to give influential messages.

People via Media as Inputs

Many of the messages we receive from people also come through various forms of media: newspapers, magazines, TV, radio, movies, music, books, and YouTube. We take in messages from the news, talk shows, podcasts, blogs, and editorials. We may know the people who are giving us messages, like our contacts on Facebook, Twitter, LinkedIn, Pinterest, and Google+. Or we may barely know the people we communicate with in online chat rooms and forums.

Advertising may be a less obvious input, but it is utterly pervasive in our culture today. It is difficult, if not impossible, to avoid it completely. It's in the mailbox, in smart-phone apps, embedded in our Internet search results, on billboards along the road, and inserted into TV shows and radio programs. Advertising is everywhere, and it's wise to be aware of what effect it's having on us, that is, on our thoughts, feelings and actions.

When we become aware of the messages we are receiving, we can note how they affect us. We can decide which inputs support us and which hinder us, and make new choices based on that information.

Why Positive Inputs Are So Important

In the chapter "The Great Exchange," we explained how our thinking, with our various mindsets, can enslave us and keep us from living our calling. This is because we first need to believe we can do something before we'll try to do anything. We must have the right frame of mind by closely examining the messages that influence our thinking in key areas like our abilities, our worthiness, and our calling. Then we can decide if it is an input we want to keep, or one to free ourselves of.

The Input Effect

Each of us needs to determine for ourselves how an input affects us. People who talk badly about other people, complain a lot, or express worry about what's going to happen tend to get us down, as does the news when the stories have a negative slant. The effect is most intense when we hear discouraging things about us. If we have any doubts inside us already, their messages can help our doubts grow. Personally, I find such negative people to be really draining because I have to use mental energy to keep my positive focus. Not that one little thing will throw me off, but hearing bummer things over and over takes a toll.

The effect of negative inputs becomes most obvious when we compare it to the effect of positive ones. Positive inputs move you toward your personal goals (e.g., hanging out with people who applaud you for determining your calling, books that empower you to apply new skills, and groups where you can accomplish goals together). Negative messages have no such benefit and can even have the opposite effect, driving us further from our goal.

Once we realize that our inputs exert a powerful effect on our thoughts and feelings, we can see how they also influence our choices, which are a natural result of what we believe and how we feel. With this clearer understanding of the effects of inputs, we can choose to plug in to inputs that help propel us forward instead of those that hold us back.

As we begin this crucial adjustment, we will move away from people who tear us down and move toward those who build us up. We will seek out people who believe in us and who genuinely care about us. We will look for others who are truthful with us because they care about our well-being. These people will be willing to say the things we need to hear, even if it's not what we want to hear. They won't be "yes people" who just tell us what we want to hear. And they won't mind calling us out on our behaviors, especially when they are not in line with what we claim to be our goals.

Dream Killers, Monkeys and Bananas

Have you ever been really excited to do something new, thrilled by the possibilities and eager to get started on it?

Then someone comes along and dashes your dreams.

> "That won't work."
> "I know someone who tried that, and he failed miserably."
> "You'll never make it."

It often comes from well-intentioned people who are genuinely concerned about our well-being. For whatever reason, they are afraid of change, or risk, or new things, and they don't want us to get hurt. However, their advice is not helpful because it comes from a worldview tainted by victim mentality, limited thinking or false assumptions.

It's happened to us. Venturing out from the known world of "employee" and moving into the mystical sphere of "entrepreneur" strikes fear in the hearts of many people. So when we shared our plans to start our own financial coaching business, some family members discouraged the idea. That discouragement came across in the things they said, how they said them, and even in the things they didn't say. We understood that they cared deeply for us and really wanted the best for us. In the past, they'd had a business that didn't work out like they'd hoped. It had been tough and draining. Based on their experience, they didn't want to see us struggle only to fail in the end.

So we stopped sharing our plans and progress with them. They were not able to give us the support we needed, and their negative input would only hurt our outlook, so we chose to connect with other positive inputs instead.

We know we're not alone in our experience. Here's a fascinating research study that shows how commonly bad experience translates to discouraging future attempts in other people (or monkeys, as the case may be).[10]

Picture a bunch of bananas on top of a pole and some monkeys who obviously want to eat those bananas. However, water from a fire hose blasts any monkey who starts to climb the pole. The blast of water is so unpleasant to the monkeys that they won't climb the pole again. In fact, the monkeys who have been blasted prevent other monkeys from even trying to go for the bananas. They tug and pull down any monkey who starts to climb the pole. Maybe they don't want their buddies to have the same bad experience. Next, all the monkeys who experienced the water blast are removed, and new monkeys are added.

Here's where it gets interesting. The monkeys, who were discouraged from climbing the pole, even though they never experienced the fire hose, prevent the new monkeys from trying to climb the pole. All the monkeys seem to understand that the bananas at the top of the pole are off limits, even if they don't understand why. Now the bananas sit atop the pole, untouched, because no monkeys will try to get them.

As you begin your journey of identifying and living your calling, don't listen to people who want to prevent you from trying. If they have ever sought to follow a dream, other people probably discouraged them before they even got started. So, while they mean well, they are operating on a set of assumptions that are seldom based in reality. Simply put, connecting to these inputs is not helpful.

Switch from Negative to Positive Inputs

Step 1 created the opportunity to begin this work on our calling by making time available to do new things. Now we need to start tearing down some barriers that could keep us from moving toward our calling. In Step 2 we will:

1. Identify the positive and negative influences in our lives.
2. Reduce our exposure to negative influences.
3. Increase our exposure to positive influences.

We get really excited about this step, because it creates powerful change and is often overlooked. It seems that most of us are unaware of all the negative messages that bombard us day and night, day in and day out. Even more, we are typically unaware of how these negative messages are truly affecting us. Becoming aware of these influences is the first step in getting rid of them and putting positive influences in their place.

Identify Positive vs. Negative Inputs

Positive inputs are beneficial for us and negative inputs are detrimental. Neutral inputs pretty much leave us the same as we were before. Remember, the effects may not be immediate, but they add up over time. One simple way for us to discern what kind of inputs we have is to use our feelings as a gauge. How do we feel after spending time with a certain person, watching a specific TV show, or reading a particular book? If it has left us in a positive place, it is an input worthy of our time. If it has left us thinking negatively or feeling down, we should limit or eliminate it.

10 Examples

Remember that direct contact with people isn't the only source of influential messages. Inputs also include the many messages we get from sources like TV, radio, and social media. Someone created all the messages that come through those different mediums. Think about it this way: when we are taking in information through any form of media, we are basically "hanging out" with the author of its message. Therefore, it's important to assess if that person is giving the kind of messages we want to receive.

Following are some examples of the differences between positive and negative inputs. Consider what kind of people you'd like to be around.

People who put us or other people down	or People who use their words to build people up
People who talk about what's going wrong	or People who point out positive things about us, other people, and what's going on
People who always expect the worst	or People who are both optimistic and realistic at the same time
People who complain all the time but aren't interested in making things better	or People who are solution-oriented and want to make things work
People who consistently put their wants and needs over those of other people	or People who display a genuine concern for us and our well-being
People who are quick to point out any limitations	or People who explore and share possibilities

People who focus on what they can get from us and from other people	or People who share of themselves
People who don't see the value of personal development	or People who encourage us to grow as they, too, work to improve themselves
People who blame their problems on other people or circumstances	or People who take responsibility for their choices and the consequences of those choices
People who assume the worst about other people's motives and intentions	or People who are compassionate and give people the benefit of the doubt

There are also neutral inputs (neither positive nor negative) all around us. We can choose to take them or leave them, as long as we can make plenty of room in our life for the positive stuff.

Once we start paying more attention to the various inputs, we'll find that getting positive messages feels really good and getting negative messages feels yucky. It's a natural inclination to want more feel-good, so let's use that impulse to motivate us to get more of the positive.

Make Some Adjustments

We found it was a big relief to unplug from negative inputs. We think you'll find the experience very liberating, too. Of course some of the adjustments we need to make are easier than others. The newscaster on the nightly news won't complain if we choose to cut out that show. Friends and family, on the other hand, may not react as well when we start putting some distance between them and us.

Have you ever noticed that it's easier to *start* doing something than it is to *stop* doing something? For that reason, we often suggest that people start one thing to replace another. It's easier to start plugging into positive inputs first, and then start cutting back on the negative ones. For example, if we are busy taking a class, meeting with a mentor, and going to a personal development group, we'll naturally have less time to spend with negative people. It's kind of like the dieting strategy of filling up your dinner plate with veggies so there's not much room left to pile on the high-carbohydrate pasta with extra-creamy Alfredo sauce and buttery garlic bread. Adding more good stuff makes it easier to pass on the bad stuff.

There are probably some negative people in our lives that we can't avoid altogether or that we don't want to completely exclude from our lives. However, we can choose to limit the amount of time we spend with these people. The book *Boundaries*,[11] by Dr. Henry Cloud and John Townsend, is a great resource for anyone who has a hard time saying "no" to people. Basically, we need to set boundaries that are healthy for us. When we find it necessary to interact with negative people, we need to be careful to monitor our own thoughts and feelings and not allow ourselves to get sucked into their negativity. We will explore setting boundaries more in Step 3.

Connect to Positive Inputs

This journey of self-preparation and personal exploration is ultimately about other people. The result of our efforts will be our own meaningful contribution to other people, to humanity. By it's nature, a calling is people-centered. In order to get ourselves into a place where we can really benefit other people, we need to connect with other people who will help us get there. The work we do in this step is important because we are building a foundation of support that makes all the other steps in the journey possible. No one can live their calling alone. It requires input and encouragement from other people who share our concerns about making a difference and living a life of significance. In Step 2, we gather positive people around us, plugging ourselves into all kinds of positive inputs, to make this journey possible.

People Who Encourage Growth

Finding a calling and living a calling will require a lot of adjustments. Most of us will need to learn new things, meet new people, and practice new skills. So it's very helpful to associate with people who encourage us to grow, and who themselves are growing.

Following is a list of places to go to connect with like-minded people who share a common interest in positive things. A simple Internet search will tell where to find these kinds of opportunities.

- Personal development groups
- Professional development groups and classes
- Interest-based social groups
- A coach or a mentor who's already doing what you want to do
- Community education classes offered by the local community college
- Classes through the parks and recreation department
- Book clubs
- Bible study groups
- Non-profits with a cause aligned with your passion
- Associations aligned with your passion

Our Focus

Our focus is also a type of input. The place our thoughts linger can affect our experience of life. Often we focus on filling our self up, and we think that we need to be filled up before we can consider helping other people.

When we bring up the topic of finding a calling and living more significantly, some people we talk to agree with this way of thinking.

Most of the time what they mean is that they haven't yet gotten out of life what they want. They're thinking, "Hey! Where's mine? I deserve more."

They figure that once they get their due, then they can relax and be generous. They say, "You know, you can't give from an empty cup."

But life doesn't work that way. Pursuing happiness before pursuing meaning doesn't work. The reason is that insignificant endeavors don't fill our cup. We will be stuck in a spin cycle looking to be filled up yet never being filled. If we are always looking to get ahead in life, or to be happy, we will get stuck in a "there's never enough" mindset.

When we shift our focus from satisfying ourselves to focusing on contributing to the world, we start to become filled, and as our "cup" becomes full, we are able to do even more, expanding our contribution in new ways. Mahatma Gandhi said it best:

> ### Mindset 3: Outward Focus
>
> Old Thinking: "I need to be happy before I help others."
>
> New Thinking: "I will find ultimate satisfaction when I am other-focused."
>
> We experience a shallow, fleeting happiness when we focus just on ourselves, doing things like traveling and buying nice stuff. When we do things that benefit other people, we experience a deeper, longer-lasting satisfaction. The key is to not wait until we're "feeling satisfied" with our own life because that satisfaction isn't going to come until we have that outward focus.

"The best way to find yourself, is to lose yourself in the service of others."

Note that you can still get burned out doing good things. We will address this later on in the book. If the thought of contributing to others makes you feel weary, read carefully when you get to the chapter on Step 5.

When John had his heart attack, we had plenty of money. We had a nice house with a view. We had purchased a new car. We were "taking care" of ourselves from most people's point of view.

Yet we weren't very happy. That time was probably the lowest point in our marriage. We both expected the other to contribute to our own happiness, and because the other wasn't putting in, we both withdrew and didn't contribute much to the marriage.

Some people would say, "See? Rich people are usually unhappy." That statement isn't true at all. Money didn't make us unhappy. Living without a meaningful pursuit made us unhappy. At that time in our lives, we weren't pursuing a calling, and while the stuff we owned was fun, it didn't provide deep satisfaction. Of course, living without money and no meaningful pursuit will make you just as unsatisfied. Money is just a tool. It doesn't make you happy or unhappy.

It wasn't until we started pursuing our calling that we learned a very important lesson: deep satisfaction in life comes when we contribute to the world and build up other people in a meaningful way.

The simple truth is that we don't get true satisfaction by focusing on ourselves. Think of it this way: whom are we building up when we interact with people? We are usually either creating some sort of result for ourselves or for others. We know that one day we will be gone. When we are engaged only for ourselves, we can sense a bit of the futility of our actions, and we aren't satisfied.

Imagine that when we engage with someone else, we paint the person we are building up with blue paint. The blue paint is just a visual to help illustrate the point. We can either paint ourselves blue or we can paint others blue.

For example, we give ourselves some cool experiences, like a tropical vacation, and so we paint ourselves blue. Then we buy some cool gadgets for ourselves, and add some more blue paint. Then we engage in fun activities by playing some games, or spending time in our hobby, so we add more blue paint. At the end of our life, we've piled all this blue paint onto ourselves. Then we're dead. All we've accumulated gets scattered to the wind, and the blue paint is buried with us. There's no blue paint left behind, and the rest of the world is pretty much as it was.

Now imagine that we instead focus much more on other people. We mentor someone, so we paint that person blue. We coach a soccer team, and paint the players blue. We spend some effort building houses with Habitat for Humanity or donate money, so we paint some homeowners blue. At the end of our life there will be a lot of other blue-painted folks in the world – people we have positively affected. If others have been painted enough, they may even be able to start painting other folks around them, so our results multiply. When we choose our activities and experiences, who is getting "painted", others or ourselves?

We all know deep down that focusing on ourselves ultimately leaves very little impact in the world. This is why our happiness in our hobbies and purchases are so short lived. When we focus on others, we gain a deep satisfaction. Are we painting ourselves or painting others? When we die, will the results of our life die with us, or will there be significant results left behind?

Learning

In order for us to find our calling and to be effective in positively influencing other people, we will need new ways of thinking and new ways of doing things. Being stagnant is harmful to our creativity, so let's grow ourselves in as many ways as possible: spiritually, physically, mentally, emotionally, and socially. Being a life-long learner will benefit many people throughout our lives.

There are many benefits for us, too, in being a lifelong learner. For example:

- We can maintain our mental abilities into older adulthood. In graduate school, I had a professor who said that, when it comes to cognitive functioning, use it or lose it.
- We get the satisfaction of being able to share useful information with other people. Being a lifelong learner encourages other people to learn and improve themselves, too.
- Conversations are more interesting. As Eleanor Roosevelt put it, "Great minds discuss ideas; average minds discuss events; small minds discuss people."
- We can impress neighbors and friends. Just kidding. That's not a real reason to be a lifelong learner.

"Continuous Learning" is included as a mindset because it will be an essential component of living our calling. In the book *Mastery*[2], George Leonard explains that in order to become a master at something, a person will often have to "unlearn"

> ## Mindset 4: Continuous Learning
>
> Old Thinking: "I'm done with school, so I'm done learning."
>
> New Thinking: "I'm a lifelong learner."
>
> Living our calling will require us to learn many new things like new ways of thinking, new ways of expressing ourselves, and new ways of doing things to name a few. It takes some humility to admit that we don't know it all, but no one person really can know everything. Having a continuous learning mindset will allow us to always improve our effectiveness in our calling.

what they already know and learn to do that thing in a different way. The willingness to learn anew is the only way to break through a knowledge or performance barrier. For example, Tiger Woods had to completely unlearn his swing and learn it again in a different way in order to become a master at golf.

Reading books is a simple way to keep learning. Stanley and Danko, authors of *The Millionaire Next Door*[13], found that millionaires typically read on average one nonfiction book a month. Considering that many people never crack open another book after graduating from school, that's a lot of learning on a regular basis. Here are some of our favorite books regarding human behavior and personal development:

- *The Bible*
- *Emotional Intelligence 2.0* by Travis Bradberry, Jean Greaves and Patrick Lencioni
- *The Fifth Discipline* by Peter Senge
- *Leadership and Self-Deception* by the Arbinger Institute
- *The 7 Habits of Highly Effective People* by Stephen Covey
- *StrengthsFinder 2.0* by Tom Rath
- *The Total Money Makeover* by Dave Ramsey
- *Switch: How to Change Things When Change Is Hard* by Chip and Dan Heath

Be Intentional about Media in Your Life

It's important to be aware of what messages we are feeding our minds through the various forms of media. Just as we've been doing with other inputs in our lives, we need to identify which media inputs are positive and which ones are negative, reduce our exposure to any negative media, and increase our exposure to positive media. We have a lot more power than we realize when it comes to letting messages into our lives via media. Here are a few examples of how we can reduce our exposure to negative forms of media:

TV

Truthfully, it's hard to find good TV programs that are positive that don't include killing, lying, cheating, stealing, and victim thinking.

How many times have we heard, "I didn't have a choice," in a TV program?

Did you know there is such a strong need for positive TV, yet such a lack of good programming, that many teen boys and young adult men have resorted to watching a cartoon with little pastel ponies that was originally created for young girls? Doctors Patrick Edwards and Marsha H. Redden[14] studied this growing group of males, average age 21, who are devoted fans of *My Little Pony* and who proudly call themselves "Bronies." Bronies say they like *My Little Pony* so much because, unlike most other TV programs, it is positive, shows giving reciprocal relationships, and has good moral lessons.

News

We heard from a former TV news anchor that news producers' primary goal is to provoke outrage in their viewers. The negativity in news stories, therefore, tends to be amplified greatly. Let's reserve our outrage for things that are meaningful to us, perhaps things that are related to our calling, so we can focus our energy toward the problem in productive ways.

Social Media

We don't need to know every bummer thing that happened to someone just because they like to post on Facebook frequently. Their world-view is tainted so they only see the negative things and none of the positive things that are all around. We can change the settings to hide comments from our negative friends on Facebook.

Radio

Some of us wake up to a radio show each morning without considering if that show is filling our minds with negative or positive images. Many radio shows have a negative tinge to them, whether it's an obnoxious DJ, opinionated show host, brief newscasts, or tasteless advertising.

Advertising

The effects of advertising are subtle, but they add up over time, inspiring dissatisfaction and leaving us in a perpetual state of wanting. Reducing exposure to advertising helps promote more satisfaction in life. If we cut out regular TV and radio, we've already done a lot to reduce our exposure to advertising. There are additional ways to cut back on ads. We can unsubscribe from email marketing lists. We can crank up the spam filter on the email and the pop-up ad blocker for the Internet. We can also add our phone numbers to the federal "do not call" registry. It is OK to throw away mailed ads without reading them; we'll be able to find a good deal with a little research when we decide we're ready to make a purchase.

I (Rena) recently changed what radio station I listen to in the morning. Although I like the style of music of a local station better than a similar nationally-syndicated radio show, I couldn't stand the advertisements anymore, especially a car dealer who tries to get his business name stuck in listeners' minds by saying it repeatedly in a ridiculously obnoxious way, and the bankruptcy lawyers who use manipulative, heart-wrenching stories to inspire fear in order to drum up business. Now I listen to a station that rightly describes itself as "positive and encouraging." I find it's a much better way for me to start my day.

Good Media

Not all media is bad. With a little effort, we can find and plug into positive media sources to support us on the journey toward our calling. Here are examples of media that can be positive inputs:

- Self-help books
- Educational audio books

- Video documentaries
- TED Talks
- Radio and TV talk shows focusing on personal development
- Podcasts with useful information
- Blogs that challenge us

We can even use social media tools like Facebook and Twitter to connect with big-name personal development "gurus" and learn from them for free. A simple Internet search can reveal a wealth of useful resources to plug into as we seek to replace negative media inputs with positive ones.

Our Spouse as a Positive Input

For many of us, our spouse is one of the strongest inputs in our life. It may be because of all the important things we have in common, such as our history together and commitment to each other. Or maybe it's because of the amount of time we spend together or the way we use that time. Maybe it's our depth of intimacy and trust. The togetherness we share with our spouse affords many opportunities to influence one another, hopefully in ways that are positive and supportive.

Ideally, as a couple, we approach life together as a team. There are many important decisions we need to make together and, therefore, need to come to some level of agreement on. Where to live, what job to take, and how to use our money are just a few examples. A big part of that decision-making process is coming into agreement on what we value, because ultimately our values will determine how we use our life resources like our time, energy and money. A couple that operates as a team has a shared direction in life, shared goals and dreams, and shared activities that support those things.

Unity or Discord

In reality, couples can get by without getting into agreement on what's important to them. We found in our own experience and in doing financial coaching with other couples that there are many benefits in coming into agreement on finances, though. It creates a dramatic reduction in conflicts, as well as a deeper sense of intimacy and of being a team. Personal finances are not just about money. They are a reflection of our goals, values and dreams. Some couples keep their finances separated or have only one spouse make all the decisions. Maintaining such a separation prevents intimacy because it allows a couple to avoid coming into agreement on important issues, potentially for many years. When spouses combine their money and make financial decisions together, it challenges them to look closely at what's really important to both people.

In a similar way, the journey of finding and living a calling very much reflects our goals, values and dreams. As we prepare ourselves for the work ahead, we will be making many adjustments in the way we use our time, energy and money. Many of the decisions we make will affect our spouse, too. There can be heavy costs associated with pursuing a calling when our spouse is not on board with us. Rifts and wedges are likely if we charge off toward our calling without involving our spouse, and in some cases, it can even lead to divorce. It's normal to be excited about getting on with the work ahead. We just need to bring our spouse along.

If we don't involve our spouse and instead set off to do our own thing, our spouse is likely to resent the way we are using our resources of time, energy and money. These feelings are understandable, especially if we have experienced a large shift in values but our spouse has not. If we are operating on two different sets of values, we, as a team, will be about as effective as two people in a three-legged race trying to go in two different directions.

In the companion video for the book, *Not a Fan*[15], the main character had a heart attack and subsequently experienced a dramatic shift in his values. He felt compelled to use his life's resources to help other, less fortunate people. His wife, on the other hand, did not experience that change of heart (pun intended), and she really struggled with the changes her husband made in pursuit of his calling to help others. Downsizing their home and his spending a lot of time volunteering at a homeless center were just two of the conflicts they had to work through. The story is a great example of a person making radical changes to live a calling, but we believe that he would have been more effective if he had taken the time and effort to get his wife to agree with the importance of what he was doing.

On the positive side, handling this topic with sensitivity and care can yield great rewards in the long run. When a couple decides that living a calling is important, they embark on an incredible journey together. They share new experiences and learn new ways of thinking. Doing these things together helps them grow closer rather than farther apart, a potential consequence of pursuing different interests. They will increase intimacy, as they share their deepest desires in life. They can experience a sense of being a team regarding the things that matter most in life. They can give each other support and encouragement as they travel this journey together.

A Supportive Spouse

The opportunity to be a positive influence on the lives of other people begins at home. We have a responsibility to help our spouse understand our new perspective, and hopefully see the value in finding and living a calling. If we have had a substantial change in what we believe to be important in life, we owe it to our spouse to be open about what we are feeling, thinking, and experiencing. We must also be patient while our spouse adjusts to the changes we've already made.

We cannot guarantee that our spouse will come to see things the same way we do, but we can take steps that will make it more likely. While we continue exploring the idea of a calling and its importance, we can speak the truth of our experience from our heart, which likely will eventually strike a chord in the heart of our spouse as well.

Here are some positive steps to help your spouse come alongside you on your new journey:

1. Designate this time as a turning point in your marriage; a time to deepen your intimacy with your spouse by sharing the things closest to your heart.
2. Commit to loving your spouse, regardless of your spouse's reaction to your desire to follow your calling.
3. Be patient and understanding if your spouse has a hard time with the whole idea, especially if it is radically different from the way you were doing life together before.
4. Make it a high priority to spend time alone with your spouse and explore deeper, more meaningful things together.

John and I have a coffee date every week so we can connect on a different level than we normally do on a day-to-day basis. It's a time when we're not coordinating schedules, discussing finances, or talking about the kids. Instead, we often read together, and we talk about what we've been learning. Sometimes we evaluate how things are going from a big-picture perspective. We may consider, for example, how we are doing on our family goals or on our personal goals. It's a blessing to have that special time, uninterrupted by our kids, where we can have a focused, in-depth conversation about the things that really matter to us. It reinforces our sense of being a team; we are not just going through life each of us on our own. We really look forward to our time each week.

Here are some questions you can use to explore with your spouse the idea of a calling and the importance of making a difference in the world:

- Who has been a strong, positive influence in your life? How are you different because of that person or those people?
- On whose life have you had a strong, positive influence? Whose life is better because of you?
- If you knew your life was about to end, as you reviewed your life, how might you feel about your relationships? Your accomplishments? Your possessions? Your contributions?
- What would you want people to say about you at your funeral?
- How do you want to be remembered once you're gone?
- Assuming your life isn't about to end, what do you want to add to your life story?

A Spouse Who's Also Called

Ideally, your spouse will pursue his or her own calling, too. We recommend that couples read our book together to help in this area. Hopefully it inspires some conversations between you and your spouse to pursue your calling together. We believe everyone has an innate need to make a difference. We will explore blending two callings of both spouses in Step 5 in more depth.

Ourselves as a Positive Input

The last input we'll look at is our own thoughts. This input is a little different because it's an internal influence. It is the way we influence ourselves by the way we think. While we address various mindsets throughout this book, we'll look at just a few negative and particularly influential thought-behaviors here.

Self Talk

It is important to become aware of our own internal dialogue or 'self talk.' Not surprisingly, we can be quite convincing when we feed ourselves negative messages about who we are and what we do. Here are just a few examples of the lousy messages we may tell ourselves that would interfere with living our calling:

> "I'm not very smart."
> "I never finish what I start."
> "I always mess up."
> "I'm not good enough to make a difference."

Kim Fredrickson, author of *Building a Compassionate Relationship with Yourself*[6], encourages people to be both realistic and kind to themselves by acknowledging truth and grace. She suggests using the following sentence frame to practice giving oneself a more realistic and kind view:

> "Even though..." "Still..."

Following are a few examples that change negative self-messages to ones that are more helpful and better reflect reality:

> "Even though I didn't get good grades in school, I can still make an important contribution to other people's lives."

> "Even though there are some projects I didn't finish, I still follow through on the important things."

> "Even though I make mistakes sometimes, I'm still a lovable person."

> "Even though I'm not perfect, I am still uniquely designed to make a positive difference in the world."

When we struggle with feelings of inadequacy in our ability to live our calling, we can take a new perspective: what we are doing is not about us, it's about the other people. For example, when John and I get nervous before addressing a group, we remind ourselves that we have important information that will be a benefit to others. We focus on the people we're talking to instead of on how good (or how bad) we look as presenters. Having this right focus is not only helpful for soothing unsettled nerves, it also helps us remember what's important, which is the people we serve.

Where to Focus Our Thoughts

I think the Apostle Paul was really onto something big when he gave this advice:

> "... Whatever is true, whatever is noble, whatever is right, whatever is pure, whatever is lovely, whatever is admirable—if anything is excellent or praiseworthy— think about such things."[7]

That's a pretty far cry from the things most of us feed our minds each day. In fact, it can be pretty challenging for us to find these positive kinds of things to focus on. With practice, though, it will get easier to see the good things Paul is talking about. There are positive messages all around us. We will become skilled at focusing on facts instead of on people's many assumptions and fears. We'll take notice of actions that are noble, motives that are pure, and traits that are admirable. We will be able to train our thoughts on things that are worthy of our attention and we will reap benefits in our own lives for doing so.

The main goal of Step 2 is to fill ourselves up with positive messages so we will be able to live our calling. We must identify the negative influences that would hold us back from living our calling. They can come from within us and from our environment. Therefore, let's evaluate how other people are affecting us, whether it's media, our spouse or other people in our lives or even ourselves in the way we think and in our self-talk. Then let's put our focus on things that are positive and beneficial to us and, consequently, beneficial to other people.

Key Points

- We receive a multitude of inflowing messages from people, media and our own self-talk.

- Influences impact our creativity negatively or positively, and affect our belief in what is possible for our life.

- We need to be proactive in minimizing negative messages and maximizing positive messages.

Exercises

1. Identify the different sources of media you have in your life on a pretty regular basis: social media, TV shows, radio, movies, newspapers, news headlines, magazines, advertisements, e-mails, blogs, etc. Rate each one as either positive, neutral, or negative. For those that are negative (and maybe for some that are neutral, too) make a plan for replacing them with something positive.

2. Make a list of positive inputs you want to connect to. It may take some research before you can find what you want. Be as specific as possible (e.g., books to read, people you'd like to get to know better, classes you want to take, groups you can participate in, blogs to subscribe to, and podcasts you want to listen to regularly).

3. Complete this exercise to help you determine who's a positive input and who's a negative one, based on how their messages affect you. Make a list of the five people you spend the most time with. Rate each person based on how you generally feel after being around him or her.

1 – 2 – 3 – 4 – 5 – 6 – 7 – 8 – 9 – 10

Bad about yourself   Good about yourself

1 – 2 – 3 – 4 – 5 – 6 – 7 – 8 – 9 – 10

Unimportant   Valued

1 – 2 – 3 – 4 – 5 – 6 – 7 – 8 – 9 – 10

Insecure   Confident

1 – 2 – 3 – 4 – 5 – 6 – 7 – 8 – 9 – 10

Stagnant or stuck   Empowered to change

1 – 2 – 3 – 4 – 5 – 6 – 7 – 8 – 9 – 10

Shut down   Encouraged

1 – 2 – 3 – 4 – 5 – 6 – 7 – 8 – 9 – 10

Discouraged   Hopeful

1 – 2 – 3 – 4 – 5 – 6 – 7 – 8 – 9 – 10

Tired   Energized

1 – 2 – 3 – 4 – 5 – 6 – 7 – 8 – 9 – 10

Sucked dry   Filled up

1 – 2 – 3 – 4 – 5 – 6 – 7 – 8 – 9 – 10

On edge   At peace

4. Based on your answers to Question #3 above, build a support system of people around you.

8

J. Eldridge Taylor Jr.

Founder of "The JET Foundation"

I believe that being successful means having a balance of success stories across the many areas of your life. You can't truly be considered successful in your business life if your home life is in shambles.

– Zig Ziglar

J. Eldridge Taylor, a.k.a. "JET," was destined to be a speaker. In school, JET did all right academically, but he got "U's" on his report cards for 'Unacceptable' behavior. "I talked too much," JET says. "I got in trouble for running my mouth. It came natural to me."

In tenth grade, JET played on the basketball team. On a dare from his peers, he decided to try out for the football team. When he got out to the field, the coach asked him which position he wanted to play. Up until that moment, JET had never even thought about it. He pondered the idea for a moment, and then asked the coach which position "talks the most," The coach told him that would be the quarterback.

So JET said, "I want to be quarterback." The coach put a football in his hand, and JET threw it maybe fifty yards. So much for an illustrious career in football! But what really stood out to JET from that experience was the initial question that popped out of his mouth: "What position talks the most?"

JET used his love for talking in his future job for a phone company where he worked for 23 years. His employer saw that he had an aptitude for speaking, so JET was given the job of doing a lot of presentations. However, he did not care much about the content. JET says, "I was not data driven. I was often speaking off the top of my head."

JET had some mentors at the phone company who told him that he had a voice that needed to be heard. JET came to accept that he really did have a gift for speaking. That's when his career at the phone company really took off. He was promoted three times, each promotion involving a position in leadership and speaking.

In 2006, JET accepted an early retirement package from the phone company. In order to maximize his money, he met with his financial advisor. The advisor told JET he was his own retirement and encouraged him to consider what he wanted to do next. Since JET is African American, he told JET to go to Dallas to check out the National Minorities Supplier Diversity Council. The council encourages Fortune 500 companies to partner in business start-ups with minority groups, such as people of color, women, and disabled veterans.

JET found the experience to be really exciting. He says, "Folks were getting contracts with these various big companies including the government. So that got me thinking, 'What should I do?' I started thinking about what I was good at. I knew I was good at talking."

So he talked with the company representatives at the event, asking them about their challenges in their organizations, and what they needed in order to overcome those challenges. Many representatives expressed a need for effective training.

JET had already been doing training presentations in his current job. They covered all kinds of topics from leadership and management to dealing with difficult customers. He saw these new companies had a need he could fill, and he decided to start a training company to help meet this need.

JET says, "I had always wanted to be a Les Brown, an Og Mendino, or a Zig Ziglar. Not that I wanted to be them, but I always thought, 'Wow! What a great existence to go from city to city and be able to share some aspects of your life, and combine it with some actual research and data about how we can be successful.'"

Today JET travels around the U.S., blending his expertise in management, leadership and professional development to "train the trainer." He enjoys his work so much, he says, "Fundamentally, I haven't worked since I retired." He especially likes teaching managers how to deal with difficult people. JET has compassion for "difficult" people, since he got in trouble all the time in his early years at the phone company and was probably labeled as difficult himself.

JET says, "I can't wait to train each class. I jump in that classroom and I don't care how tired I am. As soon as the lights go on at 9 am... bam! It's unbelievable, I look up and it's already 4 o'clock in the afternoon."

JET explains how he sees the Holy Spirit working in his life. He says it's about understanding the Lord's purposes for his life, and paying attention to the opportunities that come his way as well. He doesn't believe in happenstance. By letting God lead his life, he's learned to recognize where an opportunity is coming from. He watches for an opportunity that is the right fit with what he's trying to achieve.

JET is doing multiple things now, because he recognizes the opportunities God has put in front of him. God provides for JET through his work, so he can bless young people through the JET Foundation. JET says his life's calling is public speaking and helping to transform people's lives, which is why he started his foundation. The JET Foundation molds young minds, strengthens families, and builds communities.

JET explains that launching his dream has been a process. At one point, he took some time off and did some activities to learn about entrepreneurship. For example, he joined Toastmasters International and learned how to be more effective at reaching diverse audiences, researching specific topics, and reaching out to other experts for information. JET says, "People can really get behind you when it's your passion and your dream."

JET has had to learn a lot to be able to operate a nonprofit organization: from being an executive director, to getting funding for the right academic support programs, to building relationships with other nonprofits. He tries to share an important lesson he learned working in the corporate world

"When you go after your dream, there are some things you really have to pay attention to, first and foremost being your immediate family. Make sure they're along for the ride."

with other nonprofit leaders: "It is better to be in partnership and look larger than you are, than to be in a controlled silo." He wants them to understand there is more power in combining their efforts than there is in working independently.

JET has some advice for people wanting to discover their purpose and live their calling. "When you go after your dream, there are some things you really have to pay attention to, first and foremost being your immediate family. Make sure they're along for the ride." Making big changes in your schedule and lifestyle will affect your family in a big way. It's an important lesson JET learned the hard way. JET says, "At the time, I just assumed that if I followed my dream, my wife was going to be behind me. She wasn't. I didn't woo her along with me. I didn't make it so she could see herself fitting into my dream." That mistake ultimately led to a divorce, and JET doesn't want other people to make the same mistake.

For Christians like himself, JET says, "If you're a believer, get the Lord in the driver's seat every step of the way. Second, understand what it is you want to do, and pray for it. Ask for it, and let the Lord do the rest. Be in tune with the Holy Spirit and recognize when opportunities come your way. Also recognize that not all opportunities are good opportunities. That's why you need to have the Lord in it."

Finally, JET wants to encourage folks not to get frustrated in finding their calling. Some people mistakenly think that it will be easy if they are working on their dream, and that everything will just fall into place. But he says, "You got to work for everything."

He also wants to give a head's up that there will be a lot of new things to learn; what he calls "the nuts and bolts" of making your dream come true.

JET says, "Your gift is your gift. But in order to prove your gift, you're going to have to step out of your comfort zone." He recommends that people surround themselves with other great people who know more. As JET puts it, "Living your dream is important and you shouldn't do it alone."

9

Step 3: Maximize Your Energy

Replace a draining environment with a filling environment

Energy and persistence conquer all things.

– Benjamin Franklin

When we relocated back to California, John was able to transfer to his employer's office in San Jose. We were grateful for the opportunity to move back "home" and be closer to family. We were happy John would be able to keep the same job. We chose to settle about three hours away from Silicon Valley, so each week John stayed four days in San Jose and three days at home.

It was really hard on John living half time here and half time there. I (Rena) remember him saying that he didn't feel settled in our new home. Sometimes he would wake up at night disoriented because he was staying in different places. I knew it was wearing on him.

He also felt unappreciated at work. His ideas and suggestions were not valued. He felt frustrated at how little he was able to be innovative and creative in his work. I think his managers probably knew that the commute was hard on him. They may have noticed that he didn't fit into the company culture since he always wanted to improve things. Maybe that's why they let him go when there were layoffs.

It took about six to nine months for John to feel fully recovered from that difficult experience. In retrospect it was crazy for us to start our financial coaching business during that time. He was too drained to have the needed energy, and it was a lot more difficult than it should have been. But once his mental and emotional energy levels went back up, John was able to be much more productive. Through these experiences, we have learned how important it is to identify the things in life that are emotionally or mentally draining. Identifying these things allows for some serious adjustments to free up energy for more productive things... like pursuing a calling.

Why We Need Energy for Our Calling

Pursuing a calling is a unique journey for each person. There are no cookie cutter paths to any calling. It is a process of both personal discovery and choice. We need to have plenty of mental and emotional energy available. We need to design plans, create opportunities, explore options, and find creative solutions to problems. It's incredibly hard to be creative when we're worn out. In this chapter, we'll be looking at how we can free up the mental and emotional energy needed for this important work.

We also need enough energy to make sure we stick to the process from beginning to end. There will be struggles and frustrations along the way. There will be distractions and things that will discourage us from moving forward. Without the willingness and ability to persevere, our chances of having the impact that we want to have are slim to none. Having enough mental and emotional energy is essential.

Not Enough Energy

When we're worn out, we may have dreams of finding our calling, but we are unlikely to follow through on the things we need to do. We may have spurts of activity where we start things (e.g. look into enrolling in courses, volunteer our time, or start a blog). If we're too worn out, though, we will ultimately put the project on a shelf, hoping to come back to it later when we have more energy.

Unfortunately, reclaiming our mental and emotional energy can feel like a real challenge. The specific steps we need to take often elude us. We feel overwhelmed and stuck, unable to make progress.

The purpose of Step 3 is to reduce or eliminate mental and emotional drains. Then we can make the most of our energy and apply it to pursuing our calling. Of course, we probably can't get rid of all life's stresses. We just need to free up enough energy to take the next steps. In Step 1, we set aside at least 10 hours a week to this work. In Step 2, we replaced negative inputs with positive ones that encourage positive change. Now that we have opened up more time and support, we should be in a position to start making some great adjustments in our lives that will help propel us toward our calling. This is when things get exciting. There starts to be a real turning point in our lives.

Openness

We can sometimes get into a pattern and stay closed to new ideas and new ways of thinking. We may not even be aware we're doing it. But if we are closed to new possibilities, we limit our ability to grow to our full potential.

We should give ourselves credit for being able to discern good from bad, useful from not useful, and beneficial from harmful. Considering new ideas and new ways of doing things requires us to look at our old assumptions. This intellectual exercise can have tremendous benefits for us. Entertaining new ideas opens up a whole new world of possibilities in our minds and in our lives. We allow ourselves to consider new things because we have the power to choose to accept them, reject them, or modify them. All we need is some humility to admit that we don't have it all figured out yet, that we don't know it all.

Since you are reading this book, we can assume that you have some openness to the new ideas presented here. You can probably think back to times in your life when you tried out new ideas for yourself and decided that at least some of them were good, and that you were glad you tried them. Maybe you were surprised that some ideas worked out so well.

Here are some examples from our own lives of times we tried some new ideas—and were pleasantly surprised by the results:

We used to think that the Lutheran Church Missouri Synod would be the only church we could be a part of because we subscribe to their particular theology. We have been very happy in a community church for years now, choosing to not focus on differences of opinion of "disputable matters."

Mindset 5: Openness

Old thinking: "I can't trust new ideas or new opportunities."

New thinking: "I am discerning and let good things into my life."

We must be willing to consider new ideas in order to grow. At first, being open to new ways of thinking can be a little scary. This openness does not have to threaten our closely held personal beliefs, though. We always have the power to accept, reject or modify new ideas to make them work for us. Being open to new perspectives, ideas, and ways of doing things helps us greatly in being effective in our calling.

I (Rena) believed for years that eating whole foods is the healthy way to eat (not that my behaviors reflected that belief very well). I had concluded that was the best way to lose weight. I initially rejected the Take Shape for Life program, because in order to lose weight, I would need to eat Medifast meals for five out of six meals each day. Then a health coach told me that in my position, he would be more concerned about the health risks of carrying around the extra weight than eating those high-quality, nutritious, "processed" foods for a few months. I've lost a lot of weight by being open to that idea.

We used to consistently overspend on eating out. John would get frustrated that it was an ongoing problem. I had been asking for years to try using cash envelopes as a way to keep from overspending, but John resisted the idea. John had the mistaken assumption that we would need to pay cash for everything, including things like the mortgage. After attending Dave Ramsey's Financial Peace University, John understood that the cash was used for just a few budget categories like groceries and eating out. Then we were finally able to use cash envelopes—and what do you know? We stopped overspending on eating out immediately.

Energy Drains

As we progress on this journey, many of us experience a significant shift in our values. Although we made some adjustments in how we use our time in Step 1, we may need to make even more changes. We might need to adjust the way we use our personal resources, like money and energy, as well. Since we'll need plenty of energy for this journey, it's important to become aware of where our energy is going. Then we can assess whether things are worthwhile, or they're just "energy drains."

What is an energy drain for one person may not be for someone else. It doesn't matter if it seems like something shouldn't be a drain on us. If it is, it is. The rule of thumb for Step 3 is to identify the things that are draining your energy. Then make some changes so you can use that energy for more productive things instead.

We'll look at some of the most common sources of energy drains; draining relationships and draining circumstances. Then we'll explore some tools we can use to get some of our energy back.

Draining Relationships

There may be times when we are unable or unwilling to limit our time with certain people as we suggest in Step 2. Maybe these people are family members. Maybe they don't give us negative messages, yet, these relationships are still draining. There are many reasons why a problematic relationship can suck up our energy. How much energy it drains is usually determined by:

- How much we care for the other person
- The amount of time we spend with the person
- The severity of the relationship issue
- The amount of power or authority, if any, the person has over us

Following are just a few examples of what could make a relationship draining for us:

- We have an ongoing conflict.
- The person always disagrees with what we say.
- There are boundary issues, e.g. the person doesn't respect when we say "no."
- There are unrealistic or unexpressed expectations.
- The person is rude or otherwise disrespectful to us.
- The person is chronically self-centered, e.g. only talks about self and doesn't listen or provide any support.
- There are trust issues because of a history of broken commitments.

These kinds of issues are going to be a drain for most people. Imagine working for a boss who expects us to do more work than is possible for us to do. How about having a family member who treats us with contempt? Then there's the friend who never stops talking about herself, listening just enough to be able to say, "Yeah, that happened to me, too..." as she launches into her own story.

We'll have more energy to apply to finding and living our calling when we make some adjustments in these relationships.

Draining Circumstances

It's hard to imagine the wide variety of possible energy-draining circumstances. These circumstances are especially hard on us because we live right in the middle of them—we have a hard time seeing that there's a way out. Often, though, these energy-draining circumstances are the result of our choices. The good news is that we have the power to start making some different choices to improve our circumstances. Following are a few examples of energy-draining circumstances.

- We have a long or difficult commute.
- We're feeling unfulfilled at work or just don't like our job.
- We have money problems.
- Our calendar is over-full.
- We feel guilty for not fulfilling our commitments.
- We live in a cluttered mess: our home, our car, or our office is a wreck.

Any of those circumstances can suck up a lot of energy. Having a combination of draining circumstances is even worse. For example, we have met many people who hate their job but continue working there because they're hurting financially.

Of course, there are some energy-draining situations that are going to be beyond our power to change, such as a terminal illness in the family or a divorce. We may have to wait out these kinds of life situations, primarily focusing our energy on getting through those rough circumstances rather than actively working toward our calling.

It's important to recognize when something is genuinely beyond our control and to be OK with it. The "Serenity Prayer," which is so popular in 12-step recovery groups like Alcoholics Anonymous, offers a useful perspective:

> *"God grant me*
> *The serenity to accept the things I cannot change,*
> *Courage to change the things I can,*
> *And the wisdom to know the difference."*

The Serenity Prayer offers a balanced view of life. It reminds us to take responsibility for the things in our control, and to accept the things we truly are not able to change. Sometimes it's tricky to know what is in our power to change, so asking for wisdom to discern certainly won't hurt.

Tools for Reclaiming Energy

Unfortunately, we can't include a comprehensive collection of tools to resolve all our energy drains. Instead, we will look at three tools that can be applied to resolving many different kinds of energy-draining problems:

- Creating and maintaining healthy boundaries through communication
- The Burrito Principle for negotiating and creative problem solving
- Tweaking our environment to reduce our dependence on willpower

Communication and Healthy Boundaries

It is refreshing to realize how much power we really have in our relationships. Rather than passively accepting poor treatment, we, in many circumstances, can define what we want from the other person. By setting new expectations, we can take back energy that was getting sucked up by a relationship where someone wasn't respecting our boundaries.

To establish new expectations regarding boundaries, we need to clearly communicate with the other person:

- What behaviors are problems for us.
- If appropriate, how we feel in response to those behaviors.
- What specific behaviors we want instead.
- What the consequences will be if they choose not to comply.

We must identify exactly what behaviors are problems for us. If we speak in vague generalities, the other person may not have any idea what we're talking about. So, instead of telling our teen that he has a bad attitude when we remind him about his chores, we should tell him that he rolls his eyes, lets out a loud sigh and stomps his feet when he walks away.

Depending on the relationship, it can be very helpful for the other person to understand why we want certain behaviors to change. If the person has a reasonable level of compassion, knowing how we feel in response to those behaviors may make a big difference. Many people are genuinely unaware of how their behaviors affect us. We try our best to not blame other people for how we feel, though, because our feelings are our responsibility. So we simply state how we feel when the person behaves in that manner. Hopefully, the other person cares about us enough to not want us to have such negative feelings. If it seems like the person wouldn't really care about our feelings, it might not be worth mentioning how we feel.

Next, we need to name very specific behaviors that we want the person to have instead. It is always easier to start doing something else than it is to just stop doing something. For that reason, we request very specific behaviors from the other person. I (Rena) often think about this principle when in a restaurant I hear an exasperated parent exclaim, "Stop it!" to a child. I always wonder if the child is really clear on what she shouldn't be doing and what specific behaviors she should be doing instead. Now I know why my teachers in elementary school always told us to keep our bottoms on our seats, our mouths closed, and our hands in our lap.

Finally, the consequence we identify should be very clearly stated. It should be well thought out, rather than a knee-jerk reaction. After all, it is essential that we are willing and able to follow through on delivering the specified consequence. If we allow the problematic behavior to continue without following through with the consequence, the person will always wonder if we are serious about the importance of our request and if it is really necessary to make those changes. We tend to favor natural consequences or consequences that are otherwise logically related to the behavior, such as no longer loaning movies to a friend who doesn't return them when promised.

We're not suggesting that one should treat people like children (unless they are children). We need to set up and maintain healthy boundaries, which are important in all relationships. Following are some examples of someone setting healthy boundaries with another person:

> **Problematic behavior**: "You have been arriving 15 to 20 minutes late for our scheduled time together."
>
> **My feelings**: "When you're late like that, I feel unimportant, as though my time is not valuable to you."

Desired behavior: "I want you to either be on time or give me a courtesy call to let me know you're running late."

Consequence: "Otherwise, I will take a break from meeting with you for a while."

Problematic behavior: "Often, when I share an idea, you point out something wrong about it. For example, I said that the sky is blue, and you commented that there were a few clouds to the north."

My feelings: "I feel like I don't have anything worthwhile to share with you."

Desired behavior: "I would like it if you would identify something good about what I share."

Consequence: "If you continue disagreeing with everything I say, I will stop participating in conversations with you."

Problematic behavior: "Son, you ask me several times if you can stay up late, even after I've already answered 'no.'"

My feelings: "I feel manipulated, like you're trying to wear me down to get what you want, and like you don't respect my authority."

Desired behavior: "If you have a special situation, you can ask me to reconsider my decision and tell me what's exceptional about that night. But if I say "no" after reconsideration, do not ask me again."

Consequence: "Otherwise, I will take away the option of staying up late for two weeks, without exception."

For more information about setting and maintaining healthy
boundaries, read Cloud and Townsend's classic book, *Boundaries*[18].

The Burrito Principle

It was getting late in the evening and I (Rena) had no plan for
dinner. I didn't want to fix dinner, but I was procrastinating on
asking John if we could go out to eat. I know he doesn't like it when I
don't have a plan for dinner. Plus, there wasn't money for it in our
newly agreed-upon spending plan. Finally, I just bit the bullet and
asked him, "Can we go out to eat?"

I felt annoyed and, well, almost angry when he asked me why I
wanted to go out. I mean, isn't it obvious enough? I just wanted to
eat out. But I stopped and considered his question for a moment. I
identified the primary reason for my request: I wanted something
really yummy, something less than healthy, that I'd never fix at
home.

To my surprise, John suggested that we go get something for me to
eat and bring it home. He and the boys could eat leftovers. It was
brilliant! I got exactly what I wanted; a taqueria-style burrito the size
of a newborn baby and a Coke, and it only cost $8.50. It would have
cost about $40 for the whole family to eat out. I was thrilled with my
dinner, and John was happy we didn't blow the budget out of the
water. It was a genuine win-win solution for both of us.

That experience was a real eye-opener. The lesson we learned that
night we gladly share with you, The Burrito Principle.

The Burrito Principle states:

> *"We really want a good end result, not a specific means
> to that end."*

When there is something we want or need, we often "jump to
solutions," quickly identifying one way to get what we want. Then

we become attached to that specific means to an end, and mistakenly believe we want the means, rather than the actual end result. There are often better ways to get the end result we really want though; ways that are more efficient, achieve better results, or work better for the other people involved.

Instead of jumping to solutions, we get better results when we:

1. Hold on loosely to the first solution that comes to mind.
2. Identify what is essential about what we want to accomplish.
3. Explore multiple options for getting the desired end result.

I thought I wanted the whole family to eat out. Actually I just wanted to eat something yummy. The solution I jumped to wasn't nearly as good as the other alternative that opened up when we identified what it was that I really wanted.

Jumping to solutions can cause a lot of problems in relationships. Once we make up our mind on what we want and decide how we plan to get it, it can be difficult to get other people who are affected by our decision to want to go along with it.

Many of us choose a specific solution on our own. Then we tell other people who are affected by our decision how things are going to be. Getting their buy-in at this point can be very difficult. We are more likely to come to an agreement with other people when we bring up what we want as soon as we are aware of our want or need. Then we can ask the other person for help finding a solution that meets the needs of everyone involved.

The Burrito Principle, when applied to relationship issues, is a useful negotiating tool. First, we identify the essential components of what we want. Then we include the other person in the problem-solving process. Together, we seek a solution that works well for both of us.

Following are some examples of applying the Burrito Principle to a conflict in a relationship:

> **Problem**: Two siblings have a conflict over shower times. The older brother wants to shower early in the morning. However, the noise of the shower wakes up the younger brother earlier than he wants to wake up.
>
> **Essential parts of solution**: The older brother wants to be done with his shower before 7am. The younger brother wants to be able to sleep until 7am.
>
> **Potential Solution**: The older brother showers in a different bathroom that the younger brother can't hear from his bedroom.

> **Problem**: A wife wants her husband to be home for dinner at a predictable time so the family can eat together, but his work schedule does not make an evening meal together possible.
>
> **Essential parts of solution**: The wife wants the family to have a regular time when they can be together and interact with each other. The husband wants to have a flexible mealtime schedule on weekday evenings to accommodate his job.
>
> **Potential Solution**: The family spends 45 minutes together before bedtime doing things like visiting, playing a board game or reading a story together.

The Burrito Principle is useful in solving all kinds of problems, not just relationship issues. It helps us identify what we really want to accomplish. This in turn helps us consider a much wider selection of potential solutions. Here are some more examples of applying the Burrito Principle.

Problem: A family is planning to go to Disneyland for their vacation. However, the mom feels very strongly against spending the vacation there.

Essential parts of solution: The kids want a vacation with the excitement and entertainment of an amusement park. The mom wants an opportunity to enjoy nature.

Potential Solution: The family spends their vacation in Santa Cruz, California where the Beach Boardwalk, Great America, the mountains, and the beach are all options within driving distance.

Problem: A couple has enjoyed going on a weekly breakfast date together for years. Now they need to cut back on their spending, and the breakfast expense looks like an obvious way to save money.

Essential parts of solution: Both people want to continue having an hour or two together each week, time that is not interrupted by kids or the distractions of home.

Potential Solution: The couple continues meeting weekly for a coffee date, which gets them away from home and costs considerably less money than breakfast.

Problem: A person's cell phone breaks, and he needs to have a cell phone. However, he doesn't want to get into a long contract and pay a lot of money every month.

Essential parts of solution: He needs a smart-phone for his work, and the monthly bill needs to be about $40.

Potential Solution: He buys a used smart-phone and signs up with a mobile carrier that offers lower rates and no contracts, because the monthly bill doesn't pay for the purchase of the phone.

Winners and Losers

In their book, *Getting to Yes*[39], Roger Fisher, William Ury, and Bruce Patton describe several different ways to approach problem solving with people. Following are several of these approaches and the mindsets that go with them.

- Win: "I don't care what happens to you, as long as I win."
- Win-lose: "In order for me to win, you have to lose," or "In order to be a good person, I have to sacrifice what I want and let you have what you want instead."
- Lose-lose: "I don't care if I lose as long as you lose, too." (Ouch!)
- Win-win: "We will find a solution that works for both of us."
- Win-win or no deal: "We won't settle for a deal where only one of us wins."

> **Mindset 6: Win-Win Or No Deal**
>
> Old thinking: "I want a solution that's good for me."
>
> New thinking: "A solution is only acceptable if it's good for everyone involved."
>
> We know there are many potential solutions to any given problem. When negotiating, therefore, we might as well assume there is a solution that will benefit both us and the other people involved. Opting for win-win solutions helps foster trust because people like knowing that we have their best interests at heart.

Often, people approach working things out with others from a "win" perspective. They are dedicated to getting what they want and are less concerned about the wants or needs of the other person.

These people are often unaware of the toll that a "win" approach has on their relationship. Since going for "win" is the norm, most people are unaware there is another, better option. "Win-win" protects the interests of both people and is beneficial to the relationship.

Though many people have heard the term "win-win," it is often misunderstood. I was just talking with someone about the idea of pre-selling tickets for an event he was putting on. Selling tickets before the event was beneficial for the person putting on the event, because he would get paid whether the purchaser showed up at the event or not. He told me it would, therefore, be a "win-win" situation. I had to gently correct him. "Win-win" would mean that the interests of both people were being guarded, whereas the event planner got paid either way, the buyers only benefited if they came to the event. Not showing up would be, of course, their choice, but it wouldn't be a "win" for them. So "win-win" *doesn't* mean, "However it turns out, I'll win."

Stephen Covey, in his book, *The 7 Habits of Highly Effective People*[20], tells us to "think win-win" as Habit #4. The Burrito Principle helps make it possible to identify what both people really want. We might as well approach every problem as though it's possible to find a solution that will work well for both people. In fact, we can insist on having a win-win solution: it's called "win-win or no deal."

Approaching problems with a "win-win or no deal" mindset has several benefits. Other people appreciate that we've got their back and that we value the relationship enough to look out for their interests and not just our own. It helps build trust, and if trust has already been broken, it can help rebuild trust when used regularly. It also frees up a lot of energy that we would have used up on fighting and then trying to smooth things over afterward.

Reduce Our Dependence on Willpower

In Heath and Heath's book, *Switch*[21], the authors describe an interesting and relevant study. Research participants sat in a waiting room that had two bowls on a table, one filled with fresh-baked chocolate chip cookies, whose delicious smell filled the room, and the other one filled with a bunch of radishes. Half the group was told they could eat some cookies but no radishes. The other half of the group was told to eat some radishes but no cookies. After waiting in that room for quite a while, the research subjects were taken to another room where they were given a test: a puzzle that was actually impossible to solve.

The group that was allowed to eat the chocolate chip cookies spent about 19 minutes trying to solve the puzzle before they gave up. In sharp contrast, the group that had to keep themselves from eating the chocolate chip cookies gave up after only 8 minutes—less than half as long as the other group. Researchers concluded that self-control is a limited resource that can be exhausted.

I am grateful to the research subjects who had to resist those delicious-smelling cookies that day. Their sacrifice was not in vain if we remember and apply what the researchers learned. In order to have the energy we need to accomplish the important things in life, we should conserve our limited supply of mental energy by reducing our dependence on willpower.

Our energy is limited, so we should choose carefully how we use it. It is very taxing on us when we have to force ourselves to do things we don't want to do and to keep ourselves from doing things we really want to do. We can increase the likelihood of following through on our plans by making simple changes in our environment that eliminate the need to rely solely on willpower.

Tweaking our environment can greatly help reduce the amount of willpower we need to exert in our life. This frees up precious mental energy for the things that matter most. The following sections give some examples of tweaking our environment.

Make it Easier to Do Things We Don't Want to Do

Have you ever noticed what happens when we rely on willpower to force ourselves to do things we don't really want to do? We tend to put off those things, often making them harder when we finally get around to doing them. Furthermore, we think about how we should be doing those things when we're not doing them and feel guilty for not getting them done. Here are some examples of tweaking our environment to make it easier to do things we'd rather not do. Although the examples are specific, they can be applied to a wide variety of activities in life.

1. Make decisions in advance:

    • Choose what to fix for dinners before going shopping.
    • Set a weekly day and time to do chores.
    • Check a restaurant's menu in advance, and choose a healthy meal option before arriving at the restaurant.

2. Set up an easy win to encourage more activity:

    • Make the bed as the first step in cleaning up a messy bedroom.
    • When working through a list of calls, call people who you know will be glad to hear from you before calling people you're not as comfortable with.

3. Set up an accountability partner:

    • Arrange to work out with a friend instead of exercising alone.

- If you're having a hard time getting a project done, set up specific times to report to someone else on your progress.

4. Gather together all the needed materials in advance:

   - Fill the kitchen with convenient, healthy foods.
   - Include phone numbers on a to-do list that has phone calls on it, especially if the phone numbers aren't easily accessed in your phone.
   - Keep a file for upcoming taxes and put any tax-related stuff in it as it comes in throughout the year.

5. Make it automatic:

   - Enter phone numbers into your smart-phone, so when you need to call someone, their information is handy. Consider automatically synching this information online to prevent its loss if your smart-phone is broken, lost, or stolen.
   - Use electronic, automatic bill payment so the bills get paid even when you're on vacation.

6. Make the job simpler:

   - Get rid of excess stuff around the house to cut down on cleaning, maintenance, and repairs.
   - Combine errands and other tasks to cut down on trips.
   - Pay someone else to do the job.
   - Ditch the job altogether, if possible, by delegating, paying someone else to do it, altering your commitments, or simply deciding it's not important to get it done.

Make It Easier to Stop Doing Things We Shouldn't

We rely on willpower to keep ourselves from doing things we really would like to do but shouldn't. It's hard to pass on pleasurable things, like gooey chocolaty goodies. Making tweaks to our environment can make this less of a struggle. Following are some examples of simple changes that will make controlling ourselves a little easier.

1. Set up barriers to make indulging more difficult:

    - Use a small plate at a buffet to keep from eating too much.
    - Withdraw the amount of cash to be spent on eating out and only use that cash to pay for it to stay within your budget.

2. Remove temptations:

    - Remove unhealthy foods from the house.
    - Uninstall games from your home or work computer.
    - Temporarily turn off the cell phone, texting, email, and social media if they tend to grab your attention.

3. Make indulging less appealing:

    - Brush your teeth right after dinner to avoid late night munching.
    - Let your friends know your work hours, so if they see you procrastinating when you should be working (e.g. posting to Facebook), they can give you a hard time.
    - Set up your own consequence for indulging (e.g. for every half hour wasted, you need to make up one hour).

Make It Easier to Remember Things

We rely on willpower to make ourselves remember things. Sometimes it's stressful just trying to keep these things in mind. Even worse are the consequences we endure as a result of forgetting these things. Following are some examples of ways to make remembering easier for us.

1. To remember the essential items needed for a meeting, gather them together the night before and put them by the front door.

2. Create a checklist for to-do's and things to bring for reccurring events (e.g. camping trip packing list and instructions for the babysitter).

3. Set an alarm (e.g. on a cell phone) for reminders to be somewhere at a certain time, to join conference calls, to go to bed on time, or to pay monthly bills.

4. Pair necessary tasks with other predictable events, such as taking medications at mealtime.

5. To avoid having to search around for important items, make a home for things like keys, a purse or wallet, and cell phone.

Many of the things listed above may seem like small potatoes in the big scheme of energy-drains in our lives, but they have a cumulative effect. So, if we're fighting to stay on a diet with all kinds of tempting foods around us, we're forgetting meetings and appointments, we're forever hunting for our keys, and we're spending two to three hours a day on Facebook, we could be putting all that wasted energy to better use in our journey toward our calling. In addition to the initial energy drain, there can be a considerable loss of energy if we fail to follow through on certain things. No one likes having to pay late fees, go through the day without having enough sleep the night before, doing mounds of dirty dishes, or apologizing to a friend because we forgot about our lunch date.

In fact, all the energy drains we looked at in this step add up and take away precious energy that we need to make a real difference in people's lives. So, take the time to evaluate where your energy is going and make some adjustments where you can to reclaim that energy. You will be glad you did.

Key Points

- Environmental factors can drain our energy such as a job, certain relationships, and clutter.

- If these environmental factors are draining our energy, the result will be that we have less energy to discover and pursue our calling.

- We need to be proactive in removing or minimizing energy draining factors in our life.

Exercises

1. Consider if you have any relationships that you find draining that might be improved by clarifying some expectations.

   It may be, for example, a child, a co-worker, or a neighbor. Write out the following:

   - The name of the person with whom you have a problem.
   - The behavior you don't like.
   - How you feel when they do that thing.
   - What specific behavior you want instead.
   - What specific consequence you will bring if they don't change their behavior.

2. Identify a problem you've been facing that seems to defy a
    satisfactory solution. It could be something that's not
    working for you at home, at work or in an organization.

    Apply the Burrito Principle. If the problem only affects you,
    you can do these steps alone. If it involves someone else, you
    can use the same process together.

    •   Describe the essence of what you want. Be careful to
        identify the end rather than the means to the end.
    •   Write out a bunch of solutions that would meet that
        essential end result, no matter how silly it may seem.
        Looking at even ridiculous ideas can inspire a really
        great solution.
    •   Pick a solution that works for everyone involved. Make
        sure it is a "win-win."

3. Identify an energy drain that can be solved with simple
    adjustments in your environment.

    Maybe it's something you keep forgetting to do. Maybe it's
    time you find yourself wasting when you want to be
    working on your goals. It could be a personal habit or
    practice you've been meaning to implement. Brainstorm
    some simple changes you can make that would help you
    resolve this problem.

10

Starla McHatton

Speaking, Teaching, Preaching

If God only used perfect people, nothing would get done. God will use anybody if you're available.

– Rick Warren

Starla McHatton saw herself as a salesperson and figured she'd always be one. After all, she was really good at it.

When Starla wasn't at work, she was quiet and rather reserved. She never did anything to draw attention to herself. It's no wonder, either. When she was growing up, she was told that girls were to be seen and not heard. Naturally, being a public speaker of any kind was the furthest thing from her mind. The thought of speaking in front of a group terrified her.

One day, a woman from a nonprofit organization approached Starla. The woman's organization had a class to help people move from Section 8 housing to home ownership. The woman told Starla that she needed a teacher for the class, and she thought Starla would be the right person for the job. Starla thought to herself, "There's no way I'll ever get up in front of those people to teach."

Starla told the woman, "You don't understand, I'm not a teacher, I'm a salesman." But the woman didn't give up. She kept asking over and over. She finally said to Starla, "Look, I'd like you to teach this class this weekend. You know so much about how to move credit scores and how to invest. Whether the words come to you or not, I want you to try to teach for just thirty minutes."

Starla thought she wouldn't be able to come up with even five minutes worth of things to say. She recalls, "I was sweating. My heart was racing. I threw myself through all kinds of emotional fits and drama about doing it. But I wanted to serve her. I wanted to help people. So I said 'Ok, I'll do it.'"

The class was a small group of about 20 or 30 people. Starla bit the bullet and got up in front. About 35 minutes later, she was surprised to find that she hadn't even gotten to the meat of what she wanted to share, and she only had 15 minutes left.

The funny thing is, she was scared out of her wits the whole time. She shares, "I swear, as I did it, I was absolutely terrified. I was seeing stars. I was stuttering. I was sweating so hard, you'd think I hadn't put on any deodorant."

She was shocked at the end of the class when everyone applauded her. She thought she had done a terrible job. She had found herself thinking of all kinds of things she should have said. And she figured that it didn't matter, because she'd never teach a class like that again.

Next thing Starla knew, she was made the official teacher of the class! Normally, it would be a challenge for anyone to engage those students, because they weren't there voluntarily. Their attendance was required to participate in the home down payment grant and assistance program. Starla noticed that the students started the class half-asleep, and by the end of the class they were lined up to ask her questions and get her business card. After a few months, she was even doing business with people who had been in her class. Of all the class teachers, Starla got the best ratings from her students. Starla says, "It clearly astonished me."

Each time she taught the class, it got a little easier for her. Other people saw how good she was at teaching, but she couldn't see it for herself. Her husband, who is a pastor, told her, "Honey, you're great at this. You're a natural. This is your element. You come alive when you get up there and teach." But inside, Starla still thought to herself, "I don't come alive. I'm about to have a blackout!"

When Starla's church heard how well she was doing in teaching, she was added to the rotation of speakers. Suddenly, she had to give sermons on Sunday mornings in front of her whole congregation. She felt the same way she felt when she was first asked to teach that little class. She says that she put herself through torture and torment preparing for her first talk at church. Her husband even got a picture of her lying on the floor having a tantrum. She was kicking her legs and flailing her arms as she exclaimed, "I don't want to preach!"

But when she got up and spoke, everybody applauded. At the end, people were inspired to come up front and commit their lives to Jesus, even though the church didn't usually have altar calls. People told her that her talk was "amazing" and "absolutely incredible." They said she was really easy to identify with.

The next time Starla taught, she used sunglasses to demonstrate how a bad experience can color future experiences. To show how the effect was cumulative, she kept piling sunglasses on her face. Then she told them that God wants to take off our sunglasses. She took off all the glasses and smashed them on the altar floor. It was a great visual and it made a deep impact on people.

About a week later, she saw Brian Klemmer, a respected speaker on leadership and personal development, give a presentation at a political event. As part of his talk, he put on a great big pair of sunglasses. Starla thought to herself, "Oh my gosh, maybe I'm on to something!" It was the beginning of her accepting her call to teach and preach.

After that experience, Starla felt a stirring that she was called to preach to thousands of people someday. But not right away. For the time being, she felt the challenge to speak in front of several hundred people, if and when an opportunity presented itself.

Within just weeks, she was called to speak at a funeral. This was a totally new experience for her. She thought someone else more experienced—like her husband—should do it instead. She did not feel qualified. But as Starla puts it, she was learning that "God doesn't call out the qualified. He qualifies the called."

The funeral was for a young woman, just 25 years old, who had committed suicide. Again, Starla was terrified to speak. She recalls her experience: "Talk about feeling absolutely powerless to know what to say. When I got up, the Holy Spirit came over me. I can't remember everything I said. I think I even opened with, 'I don't even know what to say – this beautiful child...' I can't remember what I said from that point forward."

There were about 260 people there that day. Starla's declaration that she could speak in front of a few hundred people became a reality much faster than she had expected. She had pictured it as some kind of evangelistic outreach event. The funeral itself turned out to be such an event, because when the service was finished, there was an altar call. It is very unusual to have people come forward to commit their lives to Jesus at a funeral service. But that is exactly what Starla inspired her listeners to do.

Now, Starla knows she is capable of a lot more than she ever imagined. She's very grateful to her husband for pushing her to speak. He and her mentor always told her, "You don't serve the world by playing small."

On one hand, she had always had a voice inside her that was kicking and screaming and telling her, "Don't go! You may die just getting up speaking in front of somebody." On the other hand, she believes that deep inside, at some level, she must have known it was the right thing for her to do, because no one would be able to force her to do anything she didn't want to do.

She just kept getting feedback over and over from other people that she was doing the right thing. Finally, she had to admit to herself, "You're saying this, and they're saying that. So 50 people are wrong and you're right?"

"Yeah, I may do something wrong and I may do something wrong again, and that's OK.... God doesn't call out the qualified, He qualifies the called."

It took time, but Starla was able to make an essential internal shift. She moved from being overly concerned about doing something wrong or looking "stupid," to being able to say, "Yeah, I may do something wrong, and I may do something wrong again, and that's OK."

Starla says life makes more sense to her now than it used to. It's obvious to her that she is called to speak, teach, and preach. Already, a lot of people's lives have been changed as a result of her speaking to groups.

She wants to tell other people who are seeking their calling to not give up. She says, "Don't listen to the obstacles in your head. Listen to your heart. Your head is supposed to serve and carry out what God spoke to your heart. Unfortunately, we put our intellects on the throne. Your brain is supposed to help carry out your calling – not shut it down."

Three years ago, Starla was diagnosed with an incurable form of cancer. She was told that she had a 50/50 chance of surviving the chemotherapy, and that if she did, it would give her maybe another 5 years of life. She was distressed, as anyone would be. But she was particularly upset, because she hadn't fulfilled her calling yet. She prayed, "God, do not let me leave this earth without fulfilling my calling!" While doctors will only ever say that the cancer is in remission, Starla and her husband firmly believe that she is cancer free. Her passion for living her calling is what has kept her going. She declares, "That's how important a calling really is."

11

Step 4: Build Security at Home

Replace shaky ground with sure footing

I am not a product of my circumstances. I am a product of my decisions.

– Stephen Covey

A while after John's heart attack, he started talking about changing careers, possibly going to a seminary and becoming a pastor. I (Rena) remember feeling rather nervous at the thought of giving up the income of a software engineer. We didn't feel like we were living extravagantly, by any means, and it felt like money was already pretty tight. We had only a little money in savings and the typical debts: a mortgage, car loan, and credit cards. Truthfully, we didn't really know anything about reducing our lifestyle and didn't see how we could spend less money each month.

We felt stuck in our circumstances, unaware of the power we really had and our ability to make different choices with our money. It was just too scary to even consider John taking on a more significant kind of work that he wanted to do. So we continued living the same way for years. It wasn't until we took a class on personal finances (supposedly for my benefit, since John thought he knew it all) —that we acquired the tools we needed to take control of our money. We started using a monthly budget, paying off our debt and saving up for emergencies.

We felt a wonderful sense of security and peace that we didn't even know we were missing before. We finished paying off all our debts, except the mortgage, and saved up enough money to pay for nine months of household expenses. Shortly after, John got laid off from his job. The timing seemed fine to us though, as we believed God was encouraging us in our plan. John could freely move forward with doing work that would really impact people's lives in a positive way. We didn't know it at the time, but we were setting out on a journey where we would both discover our calling and live out that calling to the best of our ability. It turned out that being in a secure financial position was an essential part of freeing us up to live an other-focused life.

To begin Step 4 assumes you are already devoting 10 hours a week to your journey. You have also disconnected yourself from negative influences and connected with positive ones instead. You have made necessary adjustments in your life, so you can have enough energy to focus on this work. Doing the work required in Step 4 will further lay a strong foundation on which to build.

What Is Security at Home?

When we talk about "security at home," we are referring to having a reasonable confidence that our basic needs for things like safety, food, and shelter will be met. If we are feeling insecure or fearful in these areas, we will be very limited in what we are likely to accomplish.

Money plays a significant role in our lives. Typically, it is the biggest factor that determines our sense of security. Therefore, in this chapter we will focus on financial principles and disciplines necessary for having this sense of security. However, there are other factors regarding security at home that may need to be addressed. For example, spousal abuse, living in a high-crime area, or anticipating an upcoming job loss are all things that could create a strong sense of insecurity. Some major life adjustments would be needed first before we continue on our journey toward our calling. Otherwise, we will constantly find our energy and attention being drawn away from the work of pursuing our calling.

Why Security at Home Is Important

It is essential to come from a position of strength when we help other people. Having first taken care of ourselves, we are fortified to give to others. If we feel insecure, on the other hand, we will waver in our determination and hold back. We may frequently need to redirect our own efforts back to meeting our basic needs. Insecurity at home will undermine our efforts toward finding and living our calling.

We have seen people with really big hearts who try to help other people when they themselves do not have the kind of security we are talking about. They might be staying in a job that doesn't pay enough money because it helps other people, or they are covering the rent for someone else when they don't really have the resources to do so. People end up sabotaging their own giving potential by not first taking care of themselves. Sometimes these people will go into debt trying to maintain their situation because they genuinely want to continue helping as they have been. Ultimately, though, they experience a financial crisis when the bills and debts pile up, and the payments become more than they can handle.

Many people don't know the inner peace, strength, and confidence that come from having security at home. They may not even believe it is possible to have it. But we know from our experience—and the experience of many other people—that it's possible. Not only is it possible, it is essential for setting out on the journey toward our calling. When we first experienced this, it was an unexpected result.

Having no debt and an emergency fund helped us step out into unfamiliar territory and take new risks; ones that would have been overwhelming if we hadn't started from a place of security.

Financial Security

There is a great misunderstanding in our society about credit. Credit companies have led people to believe they must borrow money in order to do well financially. On the very face of it, it is illogical to think that having debt will be a benefit financially. The fact is that owing money adds substantial risk to anyone's financial situation.

Consider the following scenario. One person has $10,000 available credit on a credit card and no cash. Another person has $10,000 in cash and no debt. Who is in a less risky situation? The fact is that the person with the available credit and no cash will be in a very different place emotionally if there is a loss of income.

> ### Mindset 7: Financial Freedom
>
> Old Thinking: "I need to use credit to achieve my goals."
>
> New Thinking: "Being debt free gives me more freedom and opportunities."
>
> Personal money management will affect our calling. When we have money set aside for emergencies and no debt, we are in a relatively secure position financially, compared to a person who has debt and no cash. Having this kind of security keeps us from getting stuck in a bad situation, like needing to stay in a job we don't like because we need the money. It also opens up many more options for how we choose to live our calling than we would have otherwise.

When we are already in debt and are hit with an emergency, it's even worse. We could potentially lose the home, car, and any other property that has a secured loan. These things don't happen when we save up and pay cash for things.

Most people believe that having a good credit score is essential. It offers the opportunity to borrow money. A lot of people we know have continued using a credit card, believing that having access to credit puts them in a better position if they have an emergency. The truth is that having cash opens up a lot more options. The last thing you want to do when you lose your job, for example, is to go further into debt. This adds additional stress to an already stressful situation. Having cash to cover the emergency really smooths out the whole experience, allowing you to recover faster.

Another important reason to have cash available is that it enables us to take advantage of good opportunities when they come along. It's nice to be able to plunk down a few thousand dollars instead of having to say, "Wow, what a great opportunity! I wish I had the money to take advantage of it." When asked what's the most important factor in becoming wealthy, most millionaires agree that getting out of debt and staying out of debt is the most important thing to do. Having cash and no debt is a relatively secure place to be, and it leaves open the possibility of taking advantage of good opportunities when they come along.

Many people think they will keep money in savings and just use a little credit here and there. They want to maintain a good credit score and keep their borrowing options open. But the majority of people end up having debt with little or no money in savings. Studies show that people tend to spend more when using a credit card, between 12% and 18% more, compared to people who use cash. Using credit gives the illusion of being in control and of having lots of options available. In reality, using credit often limit options and harms people financially more than it helps them.

What Security at Home Looks Like

We will look at the two main components of having security at home: being debt-free and having money saved up for emergencies.

After that, we'll take a closer look at what we can do to have the necessary money to pay off debt and store up savings.

Get Out of Debt

In order to get out of debt, we have to stop using credit. Therefore, it is important to have cash set aside to cover minor emergencies, so we don't have to borrow money when small problems arise. Life happens, so we might as well be prepared by expecting the unexpected. For most people, $1,000 is a good amount to cover a broken water pump for the car, repair the a/c system at home, or cover an unexpected doctor bill. Did you know that a trip to the urgent care to get five stitches on a finger that got in the way of a knife cutting some green beans costs $500 even with insurance? (Don't ask me how I know that.) The point is: have some cash for life's little emergencies.

Once we have the $1,000 in cash, it's time to pay off that debt—all except the mortgage for now. We want to get the debt paid off quickly, so we can move on to our other goals. Mathematically speaking, it is logical to pay off higher interest loans and credit cards first, because it saves paying some interest in the end. However, we have found that it is more important for people to be able to maintain motivation throughout the debt-payoff process than it is to save a few dollars in interest. The truth is, people don't save money on interest in the end if they grow weary and discouraged in paying off their debt and give up on it. To maintain motivation and enthusiasm, we recommend using Dave Ramsey's "debt snowball"[22] method, because it gives people a quick win and shows progress very quickly.

The debt snowball method is simple. Continue making minimum payments on all debts. However, put as much money as possible toward paying off the debt with the smallest balance. Once that first debt is paid off, the money that was going toward paying it off each month can now be applied to the next larger debt, in addition to the regular minimum payment. By the time the debt with the largest balance is left, there will be a lot of money going toward it every month, getting it paid off relatively quickly. On average, highly motivated people pay off all their debt in 18 to 24 months.

Have Money for Emergencies

Once all the debts are gone (except the mortgage for now), it's time to save up money for larger emergencies. We recommend putting between three to six months of expenses in an emergency fund. Exactly how much money should be in the emergency fund depends on a person's situation. For example, if it looks like it would be relatively easy to get a new job if needed, three months may be appropriate. But if it would take a while to find a new job, six months of expenses would be better.

We know from experience that having no debt and having an emergency fund feels way better than having debt and no cash saved up. What a sense of security! We didn't know what we were missing until we were finally in that secure position financially.

Building up an emergency fund is similar to paying off debt, in that every possible dollar goes toward a savings account. Again, it's important to have a sense of urgency. Once you have established this security in your home, you will be in a far better place to venture out further on your journey toward living your calling. With a sense of urgency, most folks can save up a 3 month emergency fund in another 12 to 18 months.

Safety vs. Security

"Safety" and "security" are quite different terms, at least, in the way we use them. Safety requires taking as few risks as possible, whether it's in finances or in any other personal area, out of fear of losing something. Security, on the other hand, seeks a reasonable balance between risk and opportunity. It limits the amount of loss likely to occur, while taking advantage of opportunities that can bring substantial benefits.

Having security at home puts a buffer between us and some of life's troubles. Now, instead of fearing that we'll lose what we need, we can experience peace knowing that we have enough of what we need. We have enough money, for example, to absorb the shock of living without a paycheck for a couple months. Fear is replaced by peace, and we are able to take on more risk in other areas of our lives. We can try new things, learn new skills, and connect with new people.

The amount of risk we take in life begins with the security we feel at home. The following section gives tools and ideas for building this security as quickly as possible.

Mindset 8: Risk Management

Old Thinking: "I value safety over risk."

New Thinking: "I take appropriate risks in life."

It is tempting to play it safe in life. But if we are to do worthwhile things in the lives of other people, we must be willing to take some risks. Some risks will be personal, like trying new things, looking silly to other people, and maybe even failing at a new venture. Other risks may involve our career, our relationships, or our finances. We will be more able to tolerate these risks when we know our needs will be met and we feel reasonably secure physically, emotionally, and financially.

Take Control of Your Money

Undoubtedly, a budget is the most powerful tool in taking control of our money. It takes time and effort, but it pays off handsomely in the end.

I (Rena) was a little slower than John in understanding some of the financial principles and tools that we now use. We had been using a 'zero-based' budget for about six months when I finally really understood the power of our budget.

It was a Saturday morning. I was telling John about some item we needed to buy. I gave my pitch and waited for his response. He asked a simple question, "Where is the money going to come from?"

I thought to myself, "OK, he's not getting it. I better explain it again." So I told him about how we really needed to get this thing (I don't even remember what it was anymore). We were making eye contact, and he was nodding his head. I could see that he was listening and hearing me. When I finished, he replied, "I hear you, and I understand it's important. But where is the money going to come from?"

I stared at him blankly at first. Then I understood that when he asked me where the money would come from, he was asking which item in our budget would have to be reduced to make room for this new expense.

I remembered when we first put that budget together. We wrote our income at the top and subtracted out every item until we reached zero. We labored over it, making sure there was the right amount for every item in every category. As Dave Ramsey would say, "we put a name on every dollar." There were no dollars just sitting around that weren't already assigned to something.

I knew we had made our choices very carefully, each one reflecting our values and our goals. I knew there was no item in our budget that we would want to reduce to be able to add something new. Finally, I admitted, "Oh. We don't have the money for it." That's the moment when I really understood our budget.

Here are five essential characteristics of a budget that works:

1. **If you are married, you and your spouse agree on it.**

   If you have a budget, but your spouse doesn't agree to follow it, you might as well crumple it up and throw it in the trash. Both people must have input so that the budget reflects what values are important to each of them.

2. **It is Zero-based.**

   A zero-based budget simply means that every dollar has an assigned destination. The income is listed at the top, and all the budget items are subtracted from that income until the balance is zero. It is a common misperception that having money "left over" after all the expenses are paid is a good thing. In our experience, any money that wasn't designated to go toward anything in particular, even if for savings, tends to just disappear. John Maxwell put it well when he said, "A budget is telling your money where to go instead of wondering where it went."

3. **It looks forward, not backward.**

   As Dave Ramsey says, you need to "spend every dollar on paper, on purpose, before the month begins." Many of us have been trained to track our spending. While this is important to make sure you're staying on budget, tracking cannot take the place of creating a budget. It's essential to create the plan before any spending happens.

4. **It includes everything.**

   "Everything" means, literally, everything. There is no spending money if it isn't in the budget. There is a lot of flexibility in choosing category names and what to put under those categories. In order to include everything, it's important to include items that don't come up every month;

items you're saving up for, and any financial goals, such as paying off debt.

5. **It is easy to follow.**

    There are a few tricks that make following a budget easier. Cash envelopes are great for categories like dining out and personal spending money, where there are likely multiple purchases in the same month. It helps with making in-the-moment buying decisions when it is easy to overspend on a particular item.

Using an "itemized savings account" is great for smoothing out irregular expenses. Save money in that account for many different things, and keep track of each item's balance on a spreadsheet or sheet of paper. It's great for:

- Things you buy occasionally, like clothing.
- Bills that come quarterly, semi-annually or annually, like property taxes.
- Items whose amount fluctuates from month to month, like utilities.

How to Have More Money

Basically there are three ways to get more money: earn more money, spend less money, or sell some stuff. We've noticed that as people start making progress on their goals, they get more excited and start doing more of these activities. Following are some examples of how to get more money to increase security at home.

1. Earn Some Extra Money

    - If you are a professional, do some contract work or freelancing on the side.

- Get a part-time job as a school crossing guard or lunch monitor, waiter, or sign holder.
- Do some odd jobs like babysitting, walking the neighbor's dog, pet sitting, cleaning, or yard work.

2. Sell Some Stuff

- Sell some things on craigslist.org, ebay.com, or amazon.com.
- Host a garage sale.
- Rent out a spare room in your home.
- Sell some stuff to local shops that buy things like books, gold, clothing, movies, CD's, and video games.

3. Save Money

- Bring your lunch to work instead of eating out.
- Skip the Starbuck's.
- Wait on taking a particular trip.
- Cancel the gym membership if you can exercise enough by walking with a friend, lifting weights at home, or cycling to work.
- Give up paid services and do the work yourself (e.g. car wash, maid, carpet cleaner, lawn service, exterminator).
- Opt for free or very inexpensive entertainment: borrow books, magazines and videos from the public library, cancel cable television, and try Hulu or Netflix.
- Drink water instead of soda, or make your own instant drinks like iced tea or lemonade.
- Plan your week's meals according to what's on sale that week.

- Give homemade gifts instead of more expensive store-bought ones (e.g. a framed photo, poem, or personally made coupon for spending time together or doing someone's chore for him or her).
- Empty out your storage locker and stop paying that monthly bill.

Use the "DefCon" System to Reduce Spending

It's not easy to make our spending align with our values, or I suppose we'd all be doing it. Budgets force us to make some decisions in advance, but it's not always clear how much money we should put in the budget for each item. We're often asking ourselves how much we can "afford" to pay for something. To help with this dilemma, we created a system that makes these decisions easier and more logical. We call it our "DefCon" system. It helped us make necessary adjustments when we experienced a dramatic change in income. It allowed us to shift our spending so we were only spending according to what was really important to us. That way, for example, there was money for living a calling because the other, less important things, were not using up our money.

The U.S. military uses the DEFCON (Defense Condition) system to describe its present defensive position, when outside forces threaten U.S. security. The DEFCON status is "5" when we are at peace with no cause for increased intelligence or military activities. A DEFCON level of "1" means that war is eminent.

We apply a similar system to personal finances. Our DefCon system has five levels of lifestyle that are determined by personal values, financial goals and income level. Here's how it works:

DefCon 1   includes bare necessities.
DefCon 2   includes other necessities.
DefCon 3   includes things that are important to us, including current financial goals.

DefCon 4   includes things that are nice to have.
DefCon 5   includes various luxuries.

To use the DefCon system, write each budget category on a 3 x 5 card. Then place each card where you think it belongs on one of five piles, each pile representing a DefCon level.

The DefCon system is a powerful tool because it:

- Helps us clarify our values and priorities.
- Simplifies decisions about spending cuts if we have a reduction in our income or a goal to eliminate debt.

While there are many tricks and tips available for saving money, there is nothing quite as powerful—and simple—as removing an entire stack of DefCon cards. So while a person may have enough income to cover all the items in DefCon levels 1 through 4 and he could continue living at DefCon 4, he might instead choose to live at DefCon 3 temporarily by setting aside the cards from level 4. He could then put those categories on hold for a while as he applies the money to a financial goal, like building an emergency savings fund.

It is imperative for us to create adequate security at home as soon as possible. We want to be ready to discover and pursue our calling. Working through this process quickly requires commitment and focus. But the challenging work that we do in this step will ultimately benefit many people and allow us to be well satisfied with what we accomplished in our lifetime.

Key Points

- When we are feeling insecure at home, it will be much harder to venture out into new areas for our calling.

- It is important, therefore, to address the causes of these insecurities, which could be something like an abusive spouse, imminent job loss, or high crime neighborhood.

- For many of us, the biggest cause of insecurity is our finances.

- Getting out of debt and building an emergency fund will make us feel more secure.

- The best tool for getting control over our money is a spending plan with the DefCon system.

Exercises

1. Create a zero-based budget, with your income at the top and every expense subtracted out until all your income is accounted for. Make adjustments where necessary to make the bottom line equal zero.

2. Set up an itemized savings account and a spreadsheet or other means of tracking each item's balance. (Open a bank account if necessary.)

3. Apply the DefCon system to your own finances. Write out all your budget items, each on it's own 3 x 5 card. Place them each in one of five piles, one for each DefCon level.

4. Given your current income and financial goals, what DefCon level do you choose for yourself? Gather up the cards in any DefCon level above the level you chose. Look through those cards and see if you can remove them from your budget. Readjust your budget so it equals zero at the end.

12

Ricky Borba

Media Creator

*Don't ask yourself what the world needs; ask yourself what makes
you come alive. And then go and do that. Because what the world
needs is people who have come alive.*

- Howard Thurman

From his earliest memories, Ricky wanted nothing more than to have
people's attention and to make them laugh. While other kids were
afraid to raise their hand to go up in front and talk or volunteer for a
part in a play, Ricky loved it. There he was, right at the center of
attention!

As he got older, he began to love the art of storytelling. He says, "I've always wanted to entertain, to make movies, make television shows, write, direct, act, any way possible."

Ricky believes that storytelling—whether through a book, a movie, TV show, or even person-to-person—is the best way to reach people. Ricky feels very fortunate that he is called to produce media. He loves its potential to reach mass audiences. Ricky's one desire is to tell stories that give people hope.

There was a period in Ricky's life, though, when he wasn't so clear on what he was supposed to be doing. Between the ages of 16 and 32, Ricky had a "buffet" of jobs, everything from sales to janitorial to computers. There were 23 jobs in all, with a college degree in between. Ricky didn't know what his calling was all that time, and he hoped something would eventually "pop." But nothing stood out to him and he got bored at everything he did.

Finally, in 2008, Ricky got a job he was really excited about. Ricky relocated from Los Angeles to Lincoln, California to work as a video editor at a production company. But when the economy took a downturn, he was laid off just three months after being hired. Understandably, Ricky felt really frustrated. He had a frank conversation with God in the parking lot that same day.

"Hey, I felt like you brought me out here for a reason, and now I'm jobless!" he prayed in frustration.

In that moment, Ricky believes strongly that the Lord told him that his calling was to become a pastor. Like most people, Ricky thought that being a "pastor" meant working at a church full-time and giving sermons on Sunday mornings.

As he finished his conversation with God in the parking lot where he was just laid off, he started driving home. Less than half a mile down the road, he saw a sign for a Christian college. The next day, he enrolled in that college. Two and a half years later, he graduated with a degree in pastoral ministries and Bible theology.

During his studies, Ricky learned that to "pastor" really meant to encourage and love people. Finally, he understood that his passion for film, media and art could actually be a form of pastoring.

Ricky felt that God was calling him to reach people through media. Sure enough, just a couple weeks after graduation, he connected with a group of people making movies not far from Lincoln. It was a startup company. Ricky ended up working there for the first 19 months with no pay. It was tough financially, but he knew that was where he was supposed to be.

When Ricky graduated from college, he and his family were living comfortably in a nice home, and they had two cars with monthly payments. In order for Ricky to pursue his new calling, he and his wife chose to reduce their lifestyle a lot. They cut back on cars and got rid of all their credit card debt. For two years, Ricky, his wife, their three daughters, and two pets lived in a two-bedroom apartment. They did what they needed to do to live within their means.

Ricky firmly believes that if people truly love what they do, the money will come. It might not be "riches," but because they are good at it, other people will want them to do it for them. He says, "Now, at the worst financial place I've ever been,

"Now at the worst financial place I've ever been, knowing my calling and pursuing it every day, I've never been more content."

knowing my calling and pursuing it every day, I've never been more content. I choose to find joy in this. I know that when I get up in the morning, while the money isn't rolling in yet, the things I'm working toward are building a base and a solid foundation. Once this starts building upwards, it won't be easily shaken."

Ricky feels affirmed in his calling now that he has begun working with other media professionals. He is around people who make films and are good at it, and he fits right in. They value his ideas and take his input seriously. Ricky explains, "You can do something your whole life and have people tell you you're good at it, but when you're with a bunch of people who do this for a living and they're saying, 'Yeah, you're really good at this,' it's a watershed moment. It takes a moment like this for you to truly believe in yourself."

Ricky warns that there will be obstacles when it comes to following your calling. There are the financial challenges, for one thing. But other people can be obstacles too. We all have people in our lives who may have our best interests at heart, but aren't considering our destiny. These people tell us to get a job at Starbucks, or Barnes and Noble, or to go get a computer job. They tell us to do what we know how to do. While this advice makes sense in their world, Ricky says it makes absolutely no sense to someone who is truly confident in their calling.

Many people don't understand the value of a calling, so they certainly won't understand why anyone would be willing to pay the cost of pursuing one. In following our passions, we may feel the need to pass on a job promotion, give up financial security, or even let go of valued friendships.

Ricky says, "You're going to aggravate people who don't understand your vision. We are living in a world that has done things a certain way forever, and now we're going completely against that grain. Getting people to understand this is going to be difficult."

Even with all its challenges, the journey has been well worth it for Ricky. While most people say, "I have to" when they describe their life and their work, Ricky says, "I get to" to describe what he does.

Ricky says, "I get to write scripts. I get to make videos. I get to edit things and shoot weddings on the weekends to make some extra money. Now at 35, being able to work from home with my three daughters is worth more to me than anything else, and I wouldn't trade it for any 40-hour per week job in the world!"

13

Step 5: Discover Your Purpose

Replace doing what feels good in the moment with following a purpose and a plan

Passion is power. Feel the power that comes from focusing on what excites you.

– Oprah Winfrey

Over the years, we had numerous "discussions" about the virtues of having a personal mission statement. John had previous experience creating several of them, not just for himself, but also for other organizations. I (Rena) really didn't care about creating one. I was clear that my most important task was "to raise our boys to be Godly men." I was quite content to call that my mission statement. However, John told me it wasn't a good mission statement, because it didn't address what I'd do after the boys were grown. It seemed like it was going to take forever for them to grow up anyway, so it really didn't matter much to me. It wasn't until we were writing this book together, though, that I decided to give it a try. I tried his formula for constructing one and worked with it until I felt it was just right. This is what I finally came up with: "I inspire meaningful proactivity." For me, that little phrase summed it all up, and even included my original mission statement about my sons.

I have to admit now that there is a lot of value to having a personal mission statement (or purpose statement, or whatever you want to call it). It's insightful to have a few words that so succinctly describe who I am and what I'm about. It has helped me to be clear on what I am going to accomplish in my years here on earth as a mom and in the years that follow.

So, I'm putting it in print for everyone to see. "John, you were right about mission statements!"

The first four steps were designed to help us get into a good position to find and live our calling. At this point, we should have enough time, energy, and money to be able to focus on some personal exploration. This is an exciting time!

The process we will talk about for determining the direction of our calling came directly from my (John) experience during my heart attack. Sharing some details from my story will make the reasoning behind this process easier to understand.

John's Story Revisited

The two hard questions I asked myself came from what I experienced as a conversation with God. During my heart attack, God showed me all the things in my house, my garage, and our yard, and brought to my mind Ecclesiastes 1:1-2:

The words of the Teacher, son of David, king in Jerusalem:

> "Meaningless! Meaningless!"
> says the Teacher.
> "Utterly meaningless!
> Everything is meaningless."

All the stuff we owned, that God showed me, had no lasting value. In the grand scheme of things, all of it was meaningless. In my whole house, the only things of value were my wife and kids. I wondered if

I had put enough time and devotion into my family so they knew, by my actions, that I loved them. Did I love people well, or did I love things?

Then God asked me a question. He asked, "Why haven't you done more with your life?" It didn't feel like an accusation. This question came bathed in an incredible love. I knew that no matter how I responded, I would be accepted and loved. But the question still remained.

He brought to my mind the parable of the talents. (A talent, also called a "mina," was a coin worth about 3 months wages in biblical times.) Here is the parable from Luke 19:12-26:

> He (Jesus) said: "A man of noble birth went to a distant country to have himself appointed king and then to return. So he called ten of his servants and gave them ten minas. 'Put this money to work,' he said, 'until I come back.'
>
> "But his subjects hated him and sent a delegation after him to say, 'We don't want this man to be our king.'
>
> "He was made king, however, and returned home. Then he sent for the servants to whom he had given the money, in order to find out what they had gained with it.
>
> "The first one came and said, 'Sir, your mina has earned ten more.'
>
> "'Well done, my good servant!' his master replied. 'Because you have been trustworthy in a very small matter, take charge of ten cities.'

"The second came and said, 'Sir, your mina has earned five more.'

"His master answered, 'You take charge of five cities.'

"Then another servant came and said, 'Sir, here is your mina; I have kept it laid away in a piece of cloth. I was afraid of you, because you are a hard man. You take out what you did not put in and reap what you did not sow.'

"His master replied, 'I will judge you by your own words, you wicked servant! You knew, did you, that I am a hard man, taking out what I did not put in, and reaping what I did not sow? Why then didn't you put my money on deposit, so that when I came back, I could have collected it with interest?'

"Then he said to those standing by, 'Take his mina away from him and give it to the one who has ten minas.'

"'Sir,' they said, 'he already has ten!'

"He replied, 'I tell you that to everyone who has, more will be given, but as for the one who has nothing, even what they have will be taken away.

In response to God's question, "Why haven't you done more with your life?", I started to make excuses. First, I explained to Him all the good things I had done. I wanted to show Him that I wasn't all that bad. Of course, He already knew everything about me. So I moved on to all the reasons why I couldn't have done more with my life. I had two kids. I had a wife. We needed to eat and have a place to live. I had to work.

The response I got back was just silence. He knew that my reasons were just excuses, and He didn't need to say anything. I really didn't have an answer to God's question. It made me wonder if my life had mattered.

I thought about what might happen at work if I didn't show up the next day or any day after that. I figured they would probably feel bad for a while. Then they'd just get somebody else and life there would go on with hardly a blip. I felt like my impact in the world at that time was really small.

After several more years, I realized that my two questions, "Did I love people well?" and "Did my life matter?", really aren't two separate questions. My life won't matter if I don't have a genuine concern and love for people. When I love people through my actions, my life will matter. Both questions are about love. We refer to this kind of love as "passion." We have found that it is an essential element in any calling.

Lessons from the Parable of the Talents

This parable provides some useful guidance on what's important in determining our calling. In fact, there are three important things to note.

1. We don't own our abilities

    The servants were given money to manage, but the money wasn't theirs. Similarly, we are given our talents, strengths, and abilities, but we're not meant to just use these for ourselves. They aren't ours. We have them so we can share them with the world.

2. We determine our course of action

The servants weren't told exactly what to do with the money other than to put it to work. Rather than give specific instructions to each person, the master is looking to see what each servant will do on their own.

In the same way, we are not told how to produce the results from our life. We are expected to not just be spectators but to be players in the game of life and use what we have. I believe our creator is looking to see what we're going to do with what we've been given.

3. We have more than we think

At the end of the story the master said:

"I tell you that to everyone who has, more will be given, but as for the one who has nothing, even what they have will be taken away.'"

This statement may be confusing, since each servant was given exactly the same amount of money. What does it mean, then, when he says, "The one who has nothing, even what they have will be taken away"? I think this is talking about what each servant brought to the situation. The servants were given money, but they already arrived with character qualities, strengths, and experience. Some of the servants brought courage to take risks or ingenuity. But one of the servants brought only fear.

We also have been given our own character qualities, experience, innate talents, strengths, abilities, and passions. Like the fearful servant from the parable, we can bury our strengths and abilities. We can live in fear of making a mistake or use our abilities only for our own benefit. In the end, we will have nothing to show for it. On the other hand, we can take what we have and use it to maximum effect, producing as many deep, meaningful impacts as we can.

Whether these Bible verses hold any weight with you, or if you just want your life to matter, these results won't just happen automatically. We have to decide what legacy we want to leave, what our own unique contribution to humanity will be.

We need to be passionate about our calling, and there needs to be a love or genuine concern for the people we are helping directly or indirectly.

The Calling Compass

We developed a tool to give people a sense of direction for their calling. We call it the "Calling Compass." The Compass has three basic elements: passions, strengths, and a meaningful impact. It blends these three elements to point us in the right direction for our calling. The following Venn diagram illustrates how these three elements come together.

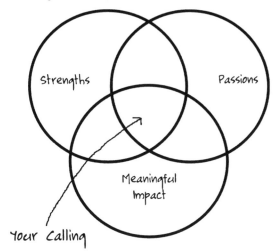

Part 1: Strengths

Strengths can refer to a lot of things. In this circumstance, our strengths are innate abilities where we are naturally gifted.

The Gallup Organization has researched and built up an entire model of strengths. Through research, Gallup has identified 34 unique, inborn talents that they call strengths. Each person has a unique mix of his or her top strengths. These top strengths influence one another to create the immense diversity we see in people. We recommend checking out some of their books and online resources[23]. The best place to start is *Strengths Finder 2.0* by Tom Rath[24].

Many people find Gallup's strengths research helpful. We have personally gotten a lot of value out of it. However, if you don't find their approach appealing, you can just pursue the things you find energizing.

Strengths Are Energizing

When we use our strengths, we get energy back. Using our strengths is fun. When we spend all day doing something in line with our strengths, we come home with more energy. Sure, we may be tired from the long day and need to rest, but we can't wait to go back the next day and do it again.

When we (Rena and I) lead a workshop or class, we are often exhausted, but we are still jazzed up. We have just used our strengths for the benefit of other people and, as a result, we feel exhilarated.

Strengths Give Us Options

Instead of limiting what we can do, our strengths open up possibilities. There can be many different ways to use the same strength. For example, a person who has the "restorative" strength loves fixing and putting things back to the way they're supposed to be. So a person with that strength might paint houses or work to rehabilitate alcoholics. These people enjoy problem solving, so they might work in a position like an event coordinator where they have to resolve urgent problems as they arise. The flexibility that comes from the strengths model makes it powerful and useful.

Strengths vs. Skills

Strengths are not merely skills. Sometimes strengths show up in our skills, but they don't have to. Have you ever been really skilled at something but you actually hated doing it? This skill isn't an expression of one of your strengths.

Our strengths are not equated to a role or position. They are more fundamental than that. For example, let's look at the role of a college professor.

Sally is a great professor. So, we might think that Sally has a talent for teaching. But teaching isn't a strength; it's a role. Rather, Sally uses her strengths that make her a good teacher. Perhaps Sally is analytical, being able to focus on details and create a logical flow for her teaching material. Being analytical helps Sally organize the class material so that students can understand it easier.

Bob is also a great professor. Unlike Sally, Bob is not analytical. His teaching style is really different from Sally's style because he draws on his "includer" strength. Bob is a great teacher because he includes all the students and makes them work together to discover the answers.

There is not a single strength for teaching, which is why effective teachers have so many different styles. Many people can use their strengths to be great teachers in their own unique way.

The same idea applies to leadership. There isn't just one leadership strength. People can lead using different styles and still be very effective.

From the professor example above, Sally, who is analytical, probably can apply her analytical strength to a lot of other situations and positions. She could potentially be a very good leader. Sally isn't locked into a teaching position by her strengths. Teaching is just one outlet for her to use her analytical strength.

When we consider how we want to pursue our calling, there are many options open to us regarding how we want to apply our strengths.

Strengths Are Not Balanced

Often we approach our life with the concept that we're only as good as our weakest area. At work, our boss will make a personal improvement plan for us to get better at something – usually an area of weakness. We spend lots of money and effort trying to become better organized, better socially, or more focused.

The truth is that we can improve a weak area only so much. If, for example, we are not musically inclined, we can spend hours and hours becoming mediocre at the piano. When we focus all our time on our weaknesses, we become average and mediocre in all areas[25].

If, on the other hand, we are naturally drawn to music, and we spend hours making up ditties on the piano for fun, it is an area of strength. We can take this natural inborn talent and go a long way with it.

The concept of being balanced in our strengths is a myth. Great football teams don't have balanced players. Each player has a specific role to play. The kicker kicks. The quarterback calls the plays. It would be disastrous to swap the kicker and the quarterback. A great team is great because the players are completely unbalanced.

When it comes to developing our inborn talents into great strengths, we should be equally unbalanced. Our strengths should be off-the-charts incredible. Our weaknesses should rate just enough so we can function when needed in those areas.

Sometimes we are taught to hold back our strengths. We are told that our area of greatest strength is our weakness. You may have heard, for example, people say something like, "That leader of ours just bowls people over. His leadership ability is a weakness. He should scale back on his leading." This concept is also a myth. The leader in this example shouldn't lead less. Instead this leader should add more compassion to his leading. Your greatest strength is not a weakness. Don't hold back.

We want to spend the majority of our time working and honing our strengths. However, there are a few times when it is necessary for us to shore up our weaknesses. For example, we may need to exchange a bad habit (like staying up late playing

> ## Mindset 9: Unbalanced
>
> Old thinking: "I need to improve my areas of weakness."
>
> New thinking: "I maximize my strengths."
>
> We will achieve the best results in our calling when we focus on and utilize our strengths. We will get very limited results by trying to shore up our weaknesses. Therefore let's just work to bring our weaknesses up to a minimum acceptable level when they are holding us back. Then we can focus on using our strengths for the benefit of other people. Working in our areas of strength yields extraordinary results, not to mention lots of personal satisfaction and joy.

on the computer) for a better habit that supports us and helps us move forward (like getting up earlier and going for a walk). Also, we should address any weaknesses in our character, because deficiencies in any area like personal integrity will hinder our efforts toward our calling. Finally, when the area of weakness involves a necessary skill or ability, we may need to get it up to a minimum adequate level. Then we can go back to focusing on improving and maximizing our strengths.

We encourage you to use your strengths every day. You will have the deepest, most meaningful impact on the world when you are using your strengths. Mediocre isn't going to cut it.

Part 2: Passions

When we pursue our calling, it needs to be something that we care about deeply. We like to think of a passion as something outside of us that consistently evokes in us a strong emotional response. The feelings we experience when we see, or hear about, or even just think about that one particular thing can be "positive," creating happiness, joy or excitement. Or it can be "negative," creating sadness or anger.

"Passions" tend to be the most baffling part of the Calling Compass for people. We may have a sense of our strengths, but many of us are not yet aware of what we really care about in life. As a consequence, we are all over the place pursuing everything at once, and nothing in particular.

We mentioned before that a calling should be other-focused. Therefore, a passion for water-skiing isn't the kind of thing we are talking about here (unless somehow there is a creative way to make water-skiing about other people). If we've devoted most of our lives so far to satisfying our own desires, we may have a hard time identifying what we care about that is other-focused.

When we work to discover our passions, we will want to dig down and find the core of the passion rather than what we see on the surface. We want to find the core "Why" of our passions, which for some people will be a process of discovery over time.

Identifying Our Passions

There are many ways to identify our passions. Here we examine five methods that we find useful.

1. **Life Experiences**

   One way to begin identifying our passions is to take a look at our life experiences. Many of us have had some intense, even life-changing experiences. Maybe it was traumatic, like experiencing the death of a loved one or having grown up hungry all the time. These experiences can make us want to help other people get through or avoid a similar situation. If we feel outraged, or burdened, or some other feeling in response to a certain situation, we are probably passionate about it.

   Similarly, we may have experienced a significant event that had an extremely positive impact on us. Maybe adopting a child rocked our world in a positive way. As a result, we want other people to have that awesome experience, too.

2. **Heartbreak**

   Sometimes we are passionate about something that breaks our heart. Possible examples include people dying of easily curable diseases, students having to share resources in a third-world classroom, or people with mental illness living on the streets.

   If something breaks our heart, it's obvious it is something we are passionate about. Maybe we're passionate because we know we can do something about it.

3. **Limited Time**

   When we consider that our life may be short, we begin to get a new perspective on things. The kind of car we drive isn't so important to us anymore, and we're not worried about looking good or appearing smart. We might not be so concerned about keeping the house clean either. We tend to become more concerned about other people and about relationships instead.

Priorities like making amends, granting forgiveness, and expressing love become super important and urgent. We may want to pass on a specific message to our kids or even to the world. If we can look at life as though we were at the end of it, the things we are passionate about become clearer.

4. **Journal and Look for Themes**

If we still aren't getting totally clear on our passions, journaling can help. We can brainstorm things that make us happy, things that we're good at, and things that we're passionate about. When we make a list of things that make our heart sing, certain themes begin to emerge. These themes can point to our passions.

Through journaling, for example, we may discover that we care a lot about an age group like kids, a social issue such as education, or an area such as leadership.

5. **Ask "Why?"**

We can use the Burrito Principle to help us discover the core of our passions. In order to find the core of the passion, we ask ourselves why something is important to us. Then we look at that answer and again ask ourselves, "Why?" Then we ask, "Why?" to the next answer we give. It shouldn't take too long for the core of our passion to emerge.

For example:

> What might I like to do to benefit other people? "I'd like to give out food to homeless kids."
>
> Why? "I'd like to help kids."

Why? "I often missed out on opportunities at school because I had to take care of things at home."

The practice of asking "Why?" has revealed a deeper passion for kids having opportunities. This simple strategy can really help us find that core passion that is otherwise eluding our consciousness.

Part 3: Meaningful Impact

We have described the need to use both strengths and passions. Many people stop after identifying the first two parts of the calling compass. But there is one essential part that is still missing: A meaningful impact.

Often, when we consider how we'll be helpful to people, we think of some form of giving. Giving is great. It helps us be more thankful and grateful and it makes us feel good. Unfortunately, though, giving does not guarantee long lasting change. Many giving projects provide only short-term benefits. We hand out Thanksgiving baskets to needy families, and these families still need Thanksgiving baskets again next year. We've solved an immediate problem, but have not changed their situation in a meaningful way.

We will cover this topic in more depth in step 7. Just remember that building our calling around a meaningful impact means that we are focused on creating long lasting, deeply positive benefits to others either directly or indirectly. This means that we are looking beneath the surface to maximize our effectiveness.

Calling vs. Charity

There is a difference between living our calling and doing charity work. Typically, our involvement in charity work will be an occasional participation in a certain charity like the Angel Tree,

Thanksgiving baskets for the needy, or coat drives for the homeless. For most people, sporadic volunteer activities are pretty much their only contribution to the wellbeing of other people outside their main circle.

Doing charity work is different than living out our calling, because our involvement in the charities doesn't have any specific focus. We'll be involved with random causes that pull at our heartstrings in the moment, and our participation will be all over the map.

Our calling, in sharp contrast, is a focused type of contribution. We'll put all our efforts into a narrow arena to make the biggest difference. The efforts we put into our calling will be clear and obvious to everyone. It will be a major theme in our life story.

Charity work is also different than living our calling when we aren't using our inborn talents and strengths. Most charity work could be done by just about anyone. For this reason, we sometimes call it "warm body work."

Mindset 10: Calling Mentality

Old thinking: "I just need to serve somewhere."

New thinking: "I use my strengths and passions to serve effectively."

Many of us have helped out various charities, but our efforts may have been unfocused and, therefore, the results we got may have been very limited. A calling, determined by our unique combination of strengths and passions, is much more focused than doing some volunteer work here and there. This focus is one of the main reasons living our calling is far more effective at bringing about long-lasting change in the lives of other people.

Our calling, on the other hand, is something we're uniquely qualified to do. It draws on our passions and strengths. Perhaps without us, the work wouldn't be as effective because we have withheld our unique contribution.

In the same way that a career is different than a job, our calling is different than charity work. Our calling is not a "warm body" type of activity. Our calling is something to which we are uniquely called. It requires us to use our special, God-given talents and strengths.

When we don't use our strengths for our calling and do "warm body" work instead, we are likely to burn out. We feel sapped. Our motivation is low, because our service feels more like a chore. When we use our strengths, on the other hand, we are energized.

Please don't misunderstand. Charity can be a great thing. It can make us more thankful and grateful for what we have. It can bring us some happiness helping out others. But participating in a charity does not replace living our calling.

No Single, Perfect Calling

Typically, we don't have just one single, perfect calling. We probably have a variety of strengths and passions that can be mixed and matched. Therefore, there are many ways we can make a meaningful impact in the world. We can choose to change our calling if, for example, we decide it's not quite the right fit for us. Or, we may choose to adjust our calling because our life situation has changed significantly. Naturally, we wouldn't change it all the time, because we want to have enough focus to really make a meaningful impact.

The Personal Purpose Statement

Our personal purpose statement describes how we apply the Calling Compass to our lives. It is a concise description of what we are all about. This statement, in essence, is our calling. It provides clear direction for us to follow. It is specific, but not overly restrictive.

Like Rena said at the beginning of the chapter, it's really exciting to have that powerful little phrase that sums up such an important part of who we are.

Over the years I (John) have created three different mission statements for myself. I've also helped create mission statements for a couple different organizations. (I think of mission statements as being synonymous with purpose statements.)

Here are some challenges I've encountered in writing these statements. Too often people or organizations create their mission statement, check it off their list of things to do, file it away in a drawer, and don't look at it again. Obviously, no purpose or mission statement is going to help us if we don't use it.

Also, when writing a mission statement, phrases can be so general that they don't mean anything. Our mission statements can become so wordy and all-inclusive that the meaning is completely lost.

Here is a horrible example of a purpose statement:

> My purpose is to be the leading expert in positive reinforcement, complementing, serving, and nurturing good will, prosperity, and happiness for the very young to the very old.

Doesn't that statement get your blood pumping with excitement? Me neither! It's important for us to avoid making a vague, overly generalized statement. It may sound official, but it's hardly going to help a person stay focused.

I have refined my own purpose statement several times. Each time, I've made it shorter and more relevant to my life. Now my purpose statement is just four words: "speaking life into humanity." If I were to guess Jesus' mission statement, I would pick from John 10:10 where Jesus says:

> I have come that they may have life, and have it to the full.

To me, my personal purpose statement has a bit of this same meaning. There are so many people who are just existing and not really living. They have jobs they don't love, want more intimacy in their marriages, struggle financially, and are just searching for the next fleeting moment of happiness. This kind of living seems like a type of death to me. And it's something I'm really passionate about helping others to change.

What Makes a Good Purpose Statement

An effective personal purpose statement must have four key elements:

1. It is short.

2. It remains.

3. It captures the essence.

4. It gives a compass heading.

Short

The key is to have a short and sweet statement that has a ton of significance to you. It may not have the same meaning to anyone else and that's okay. In the book, *The Art of the Start*[26], Guy Kawasaki suggests a three-word mantra in place of a mission statement for businesses. We recommend a personal purpose statement that is about that short, ideally just three or four words.

One of the biggest reasons to keep it short is so you can remember it easily. You want to be able to cite it (at least to yourself) at any moment. That way, if someone asks you to participate in some project or activity, you will be able to bring your purpose statement to mind quickly and assess if that project or activity meshes with your own purpose.

Shorter statements are clear and decisive. When the purpose is clear, it drives excitement. You want it to have a 'punch' to energize you to action. Remember that ridiculously long bad example of a purpose statement we shared earlier? Compare it with this one:

Developing leaders who multiply.

This statement is simple and clear. If you're into developing leaders, this purpose statement pumps you up.

When a purpose statement is longer than just a few words, it's really easy to get stuck trying to formulate the perfect phrasing. You'll spend way too long spinning your words, trying to make the statement express your purpose in just the right way to capture all the nuances. The goal is to capture the essence of the idea, not revel in perfect eloquence.

Remains

Purpose statements are not the same as goals. Goals have specific outcomes with specific time frames. Your purpose doesn't end until you are done living on this earth. Therefore, you don't want to phrase your purpose statement as a goal that may one day be accomplished. If it is written properly, you won't ever find yourself saying, "Well, I accomplished my purpose, now what?"

Your purpose statement should not be tied to any single person or organization. People and organizations come and go. Many empty-nesters have an identity crisis when their kids leave home. The purpose statement needs to outlast any particular circumstance, like being a parent, or a having a role in a particular company. Instead, a purpose statement needs to be one that remains true no matter the circumstances.

Essence

Often times, what we think we want is just an approximation of what we really want. Sometimes we think we want a specific solution, when what we really want is a deeper desire that the solution brings. This idea should sound familiar, because it is the basis for the Burrito Principle.

We need to use this same mindset to get to the root of what we really want to accomplish with our lives. Our purpose statement should never involve thinking like: "My purpose statement is *this* so I will accomplish *that*." The purpose statement is always about the desired end result.

For example, a statement like "Instructing the elderly" doesn't capture the essence if the reason we are teaching is to help the elderly to live more independently. In this case, a better purpose statement would be: "empowering seniors' independence."

Compass Heading

To capture the essence of our calling, our purpose statement will be somewhat general. Having our purpose statement provide a compass heading ensures that it's not so general that we don't know what to do.

Your purpose statement won't be specific enough to tell you what to do this week. It doesn't provide an exact map for your life, but it should give you an idea of which direction to go. From this compass heading, you should be able to set goals and make plans. It will describe your calling in a way that is meaningful to you.

A good purpose statement can succinctly express your passions, your strengths, your meaningful impact, or some combination of those elements. For you, it will be so rich in meaning that it will get you moving in the right direction.

The purpose statement should not be so vague that you don't know what to do with it, and yet it's not so specific that circumstances can invalidate it.

Create Your Personal Purpose Statement

We don't stick to a strict formula for the personal purpose statement, although we do offer one later if you're feeling stuck. Specific formulas can be limiting. It's OK if your purpose statement doesn't mention all three aspects of your calling: strengths, passions, and meaningful impacts. The important thing is that your statement embodies the essence of your calling for you.

What we're saying is that a lot can be implied by the statement. If we try to capture all the nuances, we'll be back into using long, unmemorable purpose statements that don't work.

Here are examples of purpose statements that provide some clear direction:

Developing leaders who multiply

Launching inner-city kids

Standing in the gap for single mothers

Sticky teaching for ADH..., squirrel!

Connecting needs and resources

Restoring women's power

Inspiring meaningful proactivity (Rena's purpose statement)

Speaking life into humanity (John's purpose statement)

Building homes, communities and hope (a condensed version of Habitat for Humanity's mission statement)

Notice that in each of these statements, some aspects of the calling (strengths, passions, or meaningful impact) are not explicitly stated. Some of these are about the set of strengths being used, such as connecting. Some of these are about the people that are impacted in some way. Some of these may even seem vague or unclear. What matters is that your own statement means something specific to you.

Write It Down

Writing down your personal purpose statement makes it more real in your mind. Your subconscious mind goes to work on making your purpose statement a reality. When we don't write our purpose statement down, it's too easy to dismiss it. Realistically, we can even forget what it is. We might tell ourselves that we didn't really mean it. Putting it on paper and somewhere visible for others to see will solidify your intentions.

Callings, Careers and Money

While working to discover your purpose, keep in mind that your calling doesn't have to be a charity, a cause, or volunteer work. Your calling can also be your career where you get paid. Receiving money for what you do doesn't disqualify it as a calling.

It's not wrong to get paid for providing valuable benefits to other people. In fact, we wish more businesses operated this way, with a strong sense of purpose and desire to benefit people.

For Couples

As we discussed in Step 3, it's really important for spouses to be on the same page when it comes to living their calling. If married, it's possible that our spouse may not yet be ready to embark on this journey. Hopefully, though, our spouse can appreciate our heart and support us in our calling.

Ideally, both spouses will be ready to go on this journey together. Each person can have his or her own personal purpose statement. Even though each person is different, there are creative ways to blend the purposes so both spouses can work together in their calling if they want to.

When spouses talk to each other about what is on their hearts, they will likely have some similar dreams and passions, especially if they've been married for a number of years.

Since each person can connect with more than one calling by tapping into different strengths and passions, there is a good chance that couples can find callings that overlap. For example, Bob discovers that his heart breaks over inner-city kids, single mothers, and prisoners. Sally, Bob's wife, discovers that she has a passion for adoption, ending sex trafficking, and helping single mothers.

They both have single mothers in common. Now they work together to help single mothers. Their personal purpose statements don't need to be identical. They can have very different purpose statements and still work together.

Another option is to blend together two different callings in a common effort. Perhaps Pete's calling involves a revolutionary teaching method that helps people learn much faster. Perhaps Pete's wife, Barbara, feels a calling to help inner-city kids. In this case, their callings aren't mutually exclusive. Both Pete and Barbara can work with inner-city kids, bringing different strengths to the solutions. They can blend their strengths and passions into one effort.

If You're Stuck

While we aren't strict about any particular formula, sometimes one can be helpful if we aren't sure where to start. This section provides some specific guidance to create a personal purpose statement. If you're not sure how to proceed, you can give the following practice a try.

Here is the formula:

verb + adjective + your passion

The idea is that you first pick a verb, for example, "maximize." This verb should resonate with you. Other verb examples are "leading," "promoting" or "restoring." Most likely the verb that resonates with you will touch on one or more of your strengths.

Second, you pick an adjective, for example, "innovative." This adjective should also resonate with you and in many cases will hint at the type of meaningful impact you want to make. You might be creating results that are "meaningful," "long lasting," "significant," or "contagious."

Lastly you fill in a noun that describes your passion. There should be one or two words. Some examples are: "adoption," "leaders," "financial freedom," or "couples."

You should now have a personal purpose statement that captures a little bit of your strengths, your passions and the sort of meaningful impact you want to make.

Here are some examples of this form:

Reframe innovative education

Activate loving adoption

Equip lasting personal growth

Instill lasting financial freedom

To help with this process, we have included a list of verbs and adjectives to help get the creative juices flowing. Of course, feel free to use your own.

If you find that the words you like don't quite fit the suggested form, it's quite all right to deviate from the form. It is intended to help, not to hinder, so don't feel like you should be limited by it. For example, perhaps you like the verb 'support' and your passion is for single mothers. You want to provide down-to-earth practical help, so you pick 'practical' for your adjective. But 'Support practical single mothers' doesn't mean what you want it to mean, so you come up with: 'Provide practical support for single mothers.'

It's a little longer, but it's still short, easy to remember, and provides a compass heading.

Verbs

achieve	boost	clear	develop	energize
activate	brighten	coach	direct	engage
add	bring	connect	discover	enhance
advocate	broadcast	convince	distill	enlighten
affirm	build	coordinate	draw	enrich
align	call	craft	drive	equalize
arm	capture	create	educate	equip
arrange	celebrate	cultivate	empower	establish
birth	challenge	deepen	enable	exchange
bolster	clarify	deliver	encourage	excite

facilitate	improve	mentor	reconcile	steer
fan	initiate	model	reconnect	stimulate
fill	inject	motivate	recreate	strategize
find	innovate	move	refocus	strengthen
fly	insert	navigate	reframe	stretch
focus	inspire	nurture	restore	support
forge	instigate	optimize	return	sway
form	instill	orchestrate	revitalize	switch
free	instruct	organize	revolutionize	teach
fuel	integrate	paint	sculpt	tell
gather	intensify	perform	shake	train
give	invigorate	plant	shape	uncover
grow	launch	point	share	unite
guide	lay	power	sharpen	unleash
harvest	lead	preserve	shepherd	unlock
heal	liberate	produce	show	voice
hone	lift	promote	solving	warm
ignite	magnify	pronounce	spark	win
illuminate	marshal	provide	speak	woo
illustrate	maximize	purify	spread	
impart	mend	rally	start	

Adjectives

abundant	energizing	intense	organic	traditional
balanced	essential	intentional	peaceful	transparent
bold	exponential	intimate	permanent	ultimate
broad	fair	joyful	personal	unchanging
business	free	lasting	practical	uncommon
clear	fully	lively	productive	unique
common	fun	loving	professional	universal
community	genuine	meaningful	profitable	unrestrained
contagious	glorious	memorable	revolutionary	useful
courageous	gregarious	natural	satisfying	victorious
deep	hidden	necessary	serious	widespread
distinctive	holistic	needed	significant	
effective	individual	new	solid	
efficient	influential	optimal	sticky	
energetic	innovative	optimistic	timely	

Key Points

- We each have a calling.
- Our calling is at the intersection of our strengths, our passions, and what makes a meaningful impact in the world.
- Our purpose statement will put words to our calling and give us a compass heading in life.

- Couples should talk about changes in the family culture as one or both decide to pursue their passions.

- Couples can blend their callings and often collaborate their efforts.

Exercises

1. Pick up a copy of Strengths Finder 2.0 and take the online inventory.

2. If you don't want to use the Strengths Finder inventory, Write down five to seven things that you're good at, that you like doing, and that give you energy.

3. Discover your passions with one or more of the methods below. Remember, you are looking for things that consistently evoke an intense emotional reaction in you.

Life Experience

Have you had an experience in your life where you can get excited about helping others going through the same or similar experience?

Heartbreak

Is there something that just breaks your heart?

Limited Time

Imagine you know you are going to die in a year or less. What would you want to get done before your time here is complete?

Find Themes

Sometimes you just need to start with something. Write down some ideas even if you suspect they won't be right.

The goal here is to write down five or more answers to the question, "What will make my heart sing?" Then look to see if there are any themes that appear.

Ask 'Why?'

Get to the core of your passions by asking yourself, "Why?" over and over.

4. Write your personal purpose statement.

14

Nancy Ryan

Therapist

Courage is what it takes to stand up and speak; courage is also what it takes to sit down and listen.

– Winston Churchill

Nancy Ryan had a less than ideal childhood. As an adult, she spent years working to resolve her childhood issues. She did a lot of therapy and participated in recovery groups. She needed to find out who she really was and learn how to connect with people.

Nancy felt she had not been given the basic tools needed to navigate through life. She admits, "I got really frustrated and angry about it, and I made a lot of bad choices. I asked, 'Why do I have to go through life this way?'"

As a young adult, Nancy didn't know what she wanted to do. She took some community college classes but didn't have a clear goal in mind. She went through the book, *What Color is Your Parachute?*, but still couldn't figure out where she fit in.

Nancy spent years working in sales. She was good at this job because she had become a real "people person." She explains, "I am kind to people, and I ask a lot of good questions. Curiosity has always been one of my strengths." After a few years, though, she had to admit to herself that a job in sales wasn't the right work for her. In fact, she says she hated it. She was tired of "selling widgets" and wanted to make a long-lasting, even "eternal," difference in the lives of other people.

As Nancy continued her personal growth efforts, she began to experience more intimacy in her friendships. She started hearing from friends that she was a really good listener. They said things like, "Being with you is like sitting next to a deep river," and "You just carry this sense that everything is OK and that I'll be OK," and "I just feel energized when I am with you." Her friends saw great potential in her, and their affirmations made her aware of the strengths and abilities she would ultimately use in her calling.

With her friends' encouragement, Nancy went back to college to finish her bachelor's degree. As a single mom, though, it was a real struggle. It was exhausting and frustrating to raise her child, work to support the two of them, and go to school, too.

When Nancy finished her undergraduate work, she found herself beginning to broaden her idea of what she could do. She considered how much she had grown over the years and what a blessing it was for her to have gone through therapy.

Finally, she decided she wanted to become a therapist. She said to herself, "Maybe I can do this. I've been helped so much by other therapists, that maybe I can do the same and give back."

Soon after, Nancy had her second child. She decided it was important to let her daughter grow up some before going to graduate school. When she finally did start her master's degree program, it was tough. She was having problems with her second husband and they separated. Nancy had to work in addition to going to school. In fact, she says that the biggest obstacle she's had to overcome in living her calling has been making money just to survive.

A couple of years into the master's program, Nancy was just too overwhelmed to continue. She took some time off and wasn't sure if she could bring herself to finish. But during that six month period, she had five different people say to her, "You're so close, you're so close. Just finish!"

Nancy experienced a "gentle nudging" on the inside to continue what she calls "the hard road." She says it was at this point that she finally understood exactly what she was supposed to do with her life.

It took Nancy three years to finish all of her graduate classes. During that time, she saw students younger than her, who were being supported financially, do the same thing in just a year and a half. They continued on to finish their 3,000 hours of internship in just two and a half years because they worked as a full-time volunteer. Nancy, on the other hand, is still working at it. She has worked for about six years, plugging away, to get her license. It has taken a lot of dedication and persistence.

Nancy expects she will get her license soon. She's almost finished with her 3,000 internship hours. She will then have two tests to take. In the meantime, she is slowly building up a private practice. She does her best to balance her full time job and the counseling work.

She's really looking forward to making the transition to working as a counselor full time.

Nancy has learned that living her calling is a journey, and the journey may take longer than she would like. She tells herself, "Just go do what you have to do to pay the bills."

Nancy loves counseling so much that she sometimes gets wrapped up in wanting to make the counseling her full time job. She's learned, however, that it's not worth it to try to force her calling to be a certain way. She says that not only is it very stressful, it's not even helpful.

After talking to a friend, Nancy realizes that God has her doing counseling part time, and that's what she's supposed to be doing for now. She's finally achieved a level of peace and acceptance about it because, she says, "It is a calling, and I don't get to decide exactly what it looks like. I get to show up. It's exciting, and it's fulfilling."

Now when Nancy counsels people, she uses deep, one on-one conversations to help people see their inner beauty, strength, and value. That, she says, is what her calling is.

> *"It is a calling, and I don't get to decide exactly what it looks like. I get to show up. It's exciting, and it's fulfilling."*

Nancy describes her work with excitement. "I love what I do. I could be stressed, I could be running around, I could feel like I'm not prepared, but when I sit down with a client or a couple, I'm totally there. I'm totally present. It doesn't matter what's going on in my life, I'm there and I'm energized. I watch miracles happen in front of me, and time flies. It's just really, really rewarding."

Through all her experience, Nancy has learned a few things she wants people who are seeking their calling to know. She warns that it is easy to be tempted to just follow whatever other people are doing. It's just as easy to want to chase after money. But it's important to start with your own values before you just start trying stuff. Nancy encourages people to listen to the quiet voice inside that asks:

"What really matters to me?"

"What are my values?"

"What am I really passionate about?"

"When I die, what do I want people to say about me?"

"What would my tombstone say that would show that I really made a difference?"

Nancy says that in the end, how many widgets we sell won't be important. Rather, what ends up being really important, usually has to do with relationships and people.

Nancy concludes, "I've been so blessed with friends who see in me what I didn't necessarily see in myself." She suggests asking people who are close to you questions like, "What characteristics do you see in me?" and "How do you experience me?" She says, "Then you need to be willing to truly hear whatever they say." If you're not yet clear on what your calling is, that's a good place to start.

15

Step 6: Learn by Experience

Replace head knowledge with experience

If you hold a cat by the tail you learn things you cannot learn any other way.

– Mark Twain

Rena and I started our financial coaching business for two reasons. First was to be a positive influence and a blessing to people. Second, to lead people to a place where they could also benefit others. Over time, it became increasingly clear that we were more passionate about leading people to live a calling than we were about teaching money management. Money is still very important, but we see it as a means to an end, not an end in itself.

So after three years of financial coaching, we decided to make a shift in our business. We now help people discover their purpose and live their calling, with finances being just one of many factors we address. We likely would not have discovered this path in our journey had we not first started the financial coaching business.

The lesson we learned is that we don't really know where life will lead us until we open ourselves to new experiences.

This leads us to our next mindset, which gives insight into the relationship between planning and doing.

Planning vs. Action

When starting a new endeavor, we often have no clue what it's going to look like. Because we've never done it before, we can't completely picture the end result, let alone create a plan to get there. So many of us get stuck. We can't create a plan, and without a plan, we can't proceed. So we sit – feeling discouraged. We can't get from here to there.

The problem is that we have it backwards. Unless we've done the endeavor before, the plan doesn't come first. The plan isn't yet fully knowable. Instead we need to activate a cycle of doing, learning, and re-planning. We call this cycle "Agile Planning." The concept comes from recent software development methods, where the problem can't be fully understood on the front end of a project.

We're not talking about giving up on planning altogether. We plan what we do know and begin working. We take initial steps towards our calling, and learn. Then we re-evaluate and adjust our plan. Then we do it again. We take the next step, we learn, and we readjust.

Mindset 11: Agile Planning

Old thinking: "I make the whole plan and then follow it."

New thinking: "The plan isn't fully knowable until I take steps forward."

Even though it's uncomfortable not fully knowing what to expect, we must be willing to set out on this journey without knowing all the details in advance. We will begin a cycle of doing, learning and re-planning. This agility allows us to take the steps we can do now, and from there, plan the next steps based on what we've learned along the way.

We will be able to pursue our calling only when we are willing to start without the full plan. If we are waiting for a plan to be revealed, we will be stuck.

Just Start

We discover our calling when we jump in and try it out. At this stage, you may still be wondering if you've really discovered your strengths and passions. You may still be uncertain about your personal purpose statement. That's okay.

You won't feel like you've found your calling until you've worked at it for a while and experienced it first-hand. Once your experience confirms your calling and purpose statement, you will finally have a sense that you've found your purpose in life.

It's also quite possible that you will start pursuing your calling and go, "Yuck! This is horrible." At this point, instead of giving up, you need to re-evaluate. Did you misunderstand your strengths? Did you misunderstand what you're passionate about? You may need to change your personal purpose statement, or you may just need to make an adjustment to your activities.

Perhaps, like we've experienced with our coaching business, you don't think "Yuck," but it doesn't feel quite right either. Maybe you find yourself drawn to something slightly different. Again, there is nothing wrong with making adjustments. Revisit Step 5, and rewrite or tweak your purpose statement as many times as necessary.

The important thing is that unless you actually begin, you won't learn important things about your calling.

Failure is Good

One of the things we've been taught over and over in life is that failure is bad. At school we do our class work and take our tests.

Then we get a passing or failing grade. If we get a failing grade, people see this as a reflection of our character. We get labeled as 'dumb.'

In the workplace, it's even worse. Often, when something goes badly at work, people look for a person to blame, and then they boot that person out of the company as fast as possible. The employees shrink back, playing it as safe as they can. Who wants to ever be the scapegoat?

Many of us are deathly afraid of failing at anything. We not only play it safe at work, we also play our life as safe as possible. We only do what we know we can do. Sometimes we only do things we've done before, or are only slightly different than what we've done. We learn and grow either not at all or at a snail's pace.

We want to be very clear: failure is good. Let's repeat that, just to let it sink in. Failure is a good thing.

Naturally, we don't want people to try to fail on purpose or to deliberately keep from putting in the necessary effort. But when we try hard to succeed and fail,

Mindset 12: Embrace Failure

Old thinking: "Failure is bad. Avoid it at all costs."

New thinking: "Failure is valuable because we learn from our mistakes."

It is normal to not get it right the first time we try something new. Many of us will avoid trying something new if there's a good chance we'll fail. When we are willing to venture out into the realm of new experiences, we will learn at a much faster pace than when we are playing it safe. In fact, failure gives valuable experience that helps us grow, experience we could never learn from a book. We will need to learn new concepts, try new things, and acquire new skills to live our calling. Therefore, we should not only expect to experience some failure during our journey, we might as well embrace it.

we have an awesome opportunity to learn. In fact, we often learn more from failure than from success.

Imagine that we are trying to start a business. Through trial and error, we gain a lot of experience. We become experts at what our customers want, and also at what they don't want. We know how to market our business, and we probably know who needs our product or service the most. We know why we are succeeding in our business.

If, instead, we were instantly successful from the get-go, we may not know exactly why it succeeded. If something changes, we likely can't repeat our success. In trying to repeat our success, we might even toss out the very attribute of our product or service that attracted people in the first place. Then we're left wondering why our business is struggling so much.

Playing it safe, only doing what we know we can do, robs us of the opportunity to learn and grow. If we do something right the first time, we probably took little to no risk, or we took way too long to do it. The lesson here is to be bold and embrace failure when it happens rather than fear it.

Comfort and Adventure

Sporadic volunteering is playing it safe. It's kind of like the charity work we discussed in Step 5, although there might be at least more of a theme to it. Sacrificing a bit here and there from time to time helps us stay comfortable, but we miss out when we stay inside our comfort zone.

Think of an action/adventure movie. The protagonist doesn't stay home and donate a few dollars to help solve the problem. Rather, the protagonist is the central figure in solving the problem.

In this same way, when we talk about pursuing our calling, we're talking about having the adventure of a lifetime. To have an epic adventure, we can't just live comfortably at home. We have to move out of the familiar and comfortable.

For example, consider Bob. He discovers he has a passion for homeless folks and believes he is called to address the problem of homelessness. Giving a couple dollars to individuals on the street corners isn't going to make a significant difference. If this is all Bob did, no one would say that Bob had a calling to help homeless folks. His life wouldn't reflect such a calling.

Imagine instead that Bob spends several nights a week at the local soup kitchen. He's getting to know the people there, and he's working on understanding their needs better. Consequently, Bob starts a transitional housing program to get those folks into a home. Other people would likely take note of Bob's activities and accomplishments and say that Bob was called to do something about homelessness.

Bob will make a difference by stepping out and doing things that aren't necessarily comfortable for him. It will require some sacrifice on Bob's part, because he will need to devote a good amount of his time, efforts, and priorities. The things he does for his calling aren't going to be comfortable or familiar.

Our desire to be safe and comfortable is likely to be one of our biggest barriers to moving forward. We need to be willing to step into the zone of the unknown. At least it will be unknown to us. We need to be willing to attempt new things. Mediocre isn't going to adequately answer the question, "Did my life matter?"

Many of us feel that our life is boring and uninspiring. The main problem is that we stay with the familiar and comfortable. When we step out, we feel fully alive. It can be uncomfortable and scary, but we will be inspired, excited, and energized.

When we fully pursue our calling, we give up 'comfortable,' so we can live life to the fullest.

Our Calling and Money

When we are pursuing our calling, there are some questions that naturally arise:

> "How does money fit into my calling?"
> "Do I need to make money pursuing my calling?"
> "What if my calling doesn't bring in money?"

Obviously, money is a necessary part of life. We may need to make money to give to our calling, or maybe our calling is a career that provides money. Whichever way it works will depend on a number of factors. There isn't only one approach that is effective.

Whether our calling is our career, or our calling is separate from our career depends on two things: our strengths and our passions.

I don't think anyone would suggest that Michael Jordan should have given up his career in basketball to pursue a calling doing something else. It's possible that we are also very excellent at our current career. We may be making great money and we like the work, and to toss that aside wouldn't make sense. In that case, it would be best to incorporate our career into a plan for our calling.

Our passions may also determine the options we have for money-making opportunities. If we're like Bob in the example above, with a calling to change the world for homeless folks, we're not likely to get many paying clients. On the other hand, if our strengths and passions are to lead leaders who multiply, these folks are probably willing and able to pay for leadership training.

Our Career Supports Our Calling

If we are using our strengths every day in a career that we find fulfilling, we don't need to stop our career to find and pursue our calling. Instead our career can provide for us and our family while we spend many of our nights and weekends living our calling, making a difference in the world.

Additionally, later in life, if we've managed our money well by getting out of debt, saving consistently for retirement, and paying off the house early, we will have our whole house payment each month dedicated just to pursuing our calling. So if we don't think we can merge our calling and our career, we can still make a pretty big impact at this stage of our lives with our finances.

Our Career Is Our Calling

When our career and our calling are the same, there is a certain synergy in our lives. Our time isn't divided. It might be that the career we've already picked fits our calling. In this case, we may need to only make a few tweaks. Maybe we will just become more intentional in our day-to-day activities.

Perhaps our current job or career doesn't fit our calling, but our calling really could make us money. Then we will want to launch a new career. Nowadays, people end up pursuing many careers in their lifetime, so switching isn't all that uncommon.

One way to tell if you're in the right career or job is to ask yourself, "If I knew I was going to die next month, what would I do?" If the answer doesn't include going to work, you should consider switching to something different. If the goal of a job is just to make money, then something's wrong.

If we've been successful in our career, we can leverage that success in helping launch a new calling. We can use our clout and relationships to build a new career – one that allows us to pursue our calling.

Tony Dungy, former coach of the Indianapolis Colts, is a great example. The Colts won the Super Bowl under his coaching in 2007. Tony Dungy is not working as a football coach anymore, but he does host NBC's Football Night in America. He is maintaining a career in football and, at the same time, is working to make a contribution to society. Tony Dungy has written *Uncommon: Finding Your Path to Significance*[27], and has issued the Uncommon Life Challenge[28]. So, before he winds down his football career, Tony Dungy is working to usher in a new phase of his life.

Retired and Pursuing Our Calling

Retirement is a wonderful season to live our calling. Even if we don't have a lot of money saved up, we have more time and options open to us. Some people might worry about getting bored after they retire, but this can be the most exciting time of a person's life. We can use all this free time to make a huge splash in the world!

Our suggestion is to go all out in pursuing your calling. Make the most of the remaining years of your life. Be intentional, love people, and make your life matter!

Goals, Big and Small

There are a lot of books available and methods described for making goals. There are SMART goals, GOAL goals, and DBE methods, to name a few. The problem with many of the "90 days or less" type of goals is that the focus is to achieve something in only the next few months. Because we're focused on short-term achievable goals, we often shrink back and set goals for what we know we can do. We stay within the familiar and comfortable.

Instead, we need to start with a Big Hairy Audacious Goal – the BHAG (pronounced "bee hag"). The BHAG should do two things. It should scare us. When we think about actually attempting our BHAG, we should be shaking-in-our-boots scared, because it's something we've never done before, and it's completely outside our comfort zone. Yet the BHAG should also make us excited. Our BHAG, especially when it's lined up with our calling (our passions and strengths), should pump us up with excitement. We're talking about a "run around the room and jump up and down" kind of excited.

Our BHAG should be in the middle of our zone of the unknown. It's normal to not know how to make plans for it. Instead, all we know is how to take the next step or two.

We've already created our purpose statement that describes our calling. From our calling, we create a BHAG that compels us forward. At this point, we may find ourselves overwhelmed, so it's also time for some short-term goals.

SMART goals can actually be quite helpful when they flow down from a higher purpose. Our SMART goals should move us closer to completing our BHAG. SMART is an acronym that stands for Specific, Measurable, Attainable, Relevant, and Timely (although some people use slightly different words for the SMART acronym).

Whether we use the SMART methodology or not, we believe that the following five factors are essential to creating short-term goals that will move us forward:

1. It is possible to accomplish the goal.

   If the goal is too far out of reach, it will feel unattainable, and we might be tempted not to try. So, the short-term goal needs to be encouraging, because it is something we can accomplish relatively quickly. The BHAG is different than a short-term goal. It has a long-term time frame that tells us we're part of something bigger than we could accomplish in just a couple months.

2. It is obvious when the goal has been accomplished.

   If the goal is too fuzzy in its definition, or there's no way to measure the outcome, we won't be able to know when we've accomplished the goal. We won't know when to stop and make a new goal. We'll get stuck and won't move on to the next step. Similarly, our BHAG also needs to be clear and specific enough to measure its outcome.

3. The time frame for the goal begins today.

    If the goal is too far away, most of us will procrastinate. For example, when we're getting close to taking a trip somewhere, our activities are pretty different than when the trip is a week away. We may only gather a few items here and there. But when we're supposed to leave the next morning at 5:00 am, we make a list of things we don't want to forget. We're very focused. We go over what we need to bring several times in our minds. We put things by the door we want to make sure gets packed in the car. In the same way, our short-term goals should pump this kind of energy into our actions. This type of focus is something our short-term goals can create in a way our BHAG can't.

4. The goal is written down.

    There is something different that happens in our mind when we write down goals, rather than just think about them. For one, it's too easy to justify ditching a goal if it's just in our head. We can tell ourselves that we didn't really mean it. Or we can forget that we created the goal. Instead, we should write the goal down, and put it in a prominent place where we'll see it often.

5. The goal helps us pursue our calling.

    We need to make sure that our short-term goals move us closer towards our BHAG. Before we create our short-term goals, we need to be aware of the calling and direction of our life. The result is that our BHAG flows from our calling and our purpose statement. Then our short-term goals flow from our BHAG. Our daily or weekly activities flow from our short-term goals. This way, we are accomplishing more and more of our calling every day.

Since our BHAG is outside our comfort zone, and our short-term goals flow from our BHAG, many of our short-term goals will probably also be outside our comfort zone. So, don't hesitate to make some short-term goals that are uncomfortable and scary.

Putting It All Together

To recap, we learn by experience. We don't expect to have it all figured out yet. But this doesn't mean we don't set goals. Here are the steps again that we need to follow:

1. Create and write down a BHAG that helps us accomplish our calling.

    We create the BHAG first even though we're still not sure about our calling yet. We need a Big Hairy Audacious Goal that is compelling. We still need to know where we're going with our calling. This BHAG will give focus to our goals.

2. Create short-term goals to try out our calling.

    We may interview people who are doing something very similar to what we want to do. We may set a goal to volunteer somewhere doing something similar. The idea is to get started so we can get a taste of what it's like.

3. Re-evaluate if this is a good fit.

    Do we like the direction we're going? Do we need to change the way we engage with people to better suit our strengths? Do we need to change the people with whom we're working? Do we need to tweak or change our BHAG? Do we need to change our calling or our purpose statement?

Most importantly, we must create our purpose statement and then take action on it. Let's not just leave it as a nice thought that we should look into someday. It would be a tragedy if, at the end of our lives, we asked ourselves if we loved people and if our life mattered, and we kicked ourselves for not taking action sooner.

Key Points

- We can't know for sure what our calling is until we gain some experience.

- We shouldn't wait for a full plan to emerge. We should start right away, expecting the plan to become clearer as we move forward.

- Our calling might provide our primary income, but it doesn't have to.

- We should write down our long term (BHAG) and short-term (SMART) goals.

Exercises

1. Find a secluded place to go and think – ideally, for a few days. Turn the cell phone off. Leave the TV off. If you are married, do this exercise with your spouse. Look at your purpose statement, and imagine yourself living your purpose statement. Create and write down your Big Hairy Audacious Goal. If you're married, make one BHAG for both of you that blends your callings together.

2. Research organizations and people already doing something similar to your calling.

3. Volunteer some time at one of these organizations, or spend a day with a person doing what you want to do. Consider

how you might need to tweak what is done to fit your strengths.

4. Find a mentor or coach who can help you explore, and evaluate what's working and what's not.

5. After volunteering for a few months, how do you feel? Can you see yourself doing this or something similar for the next five to ten years? Note that you might feel uncomfortable because it's so new and different, but this discomfort is not necessarily an indicator that it's the wrong thing.

16

Jon Acuff

Speaker, Author, Awesome!

Do not wait; the time will never be 'just right.' Start where you stand, and work with whatever tools you may have at your command, and better tools will be found as you go along.

– George Herbert

Like most people, Jon Acuff used to work regular day jobs. He says that they weren't horrible. He noticed, however, that sometimes there is more danger in having a job that's good enough than there is in having a job that's horrible. Jon explains, "A horrible job forces you to admit it's horrible and move on. A good enough job kind of woos you into complacency."

An important responsibility of Jon's work had been to share ideas. He shared them with his employer and with fellow employees because, he says, that's what he was paid to do.

Jon wasn't really feeling satisfied with his work, though, and he started writing his own blog. He was thrilled to find that people really liked what he had to say. Jon explains, "Suddenly, strangers I didn't work with, who didn't know me, who only knew the quality of my ideas, were responding."

The readers' enthusiastic response to Jon's blog was a real eye-opener for him. He says, "I realized there's this whole world out there that might be interested in my ideas." The Internet made it possible for him to easily get his ideas in front of more people than he possibly could have before. It was exciting to consider the possibilities and he thought, "Wow, this is a neat thing. I think I could really do something here."

Jon's blogging success gave him courage to venture out and try some other new things. He did a lot of freelance work for different companies and different people. Then he traveled to San Diego to spend a few days with a friend. Jon worked with his friend to make sense of how to communicate what his friend's organization was truly about. Jon says, "That was just fun. It was hard work, but it wasn't strenuous. It was enjoyable." He found himself thinking that he would love to do that kind of work more often.

Jon says he's still finding his calling. He explains that many people have a lot of misconceptions about what it's like to find one. They seem to think that they will have some kind of "Eureka!" moment when they will suddenly get a clear understanding of what their calling is.

They think it will be one specific thing, and that it will be just "perfect."

But Jon doesn't believe that is how a calling works. Based on his own experience, he believes that people find it by trying a bunch of different things. Then, after trying out ten or twenty things, a person can ask questions like, "What worked?" and "What was I good at?" and "What was natural?"

Regarding his own calling, Jon has been learning that he's really good at helping people put a "handle" on their ideas. He explains, "The world is inundated with more ideas than it's ever had before with the spread of social media and the Internet. But these ideas are hard to put a handle on." So, Jon is helping businesses, organizations, and individuals figure out how to communicate their idea in a "loud, crowded, busy world."

Just recently, Jon transitioned from working as part of a large team with Dave Ramsey to working on his own. He admits he has a lot to learn about being an entrepreneur. Jon needs to learn some practical things, like how to manage his own speaking tour and how to hire designers for specific projects.

Even though Jon has already experienced success as an author and speaker, he's not immune to fear. He shares concerns that all of us ask ourselves from time to time, "What if I can't do it? What if I fail? What if I succeed? What if people laugh at me?" Jon shares, "When I was just starting and even now, I'm not done with fear."

Just like anyone else, Jon has needed to make the time to work on figuring out and living his calling. Making time and creating space requires deliberate effort. "We're all pretty busy," he says. He explains that one of the simplest obstacles to living our calling, then, is our belief that we don't have time for it. For Jon, he had to start with admitting that there were ways he could free up more time in his life.

To other people seeking to discover their purpose and live their calling, he says, "I would tell them to practice. I think sometimes we want to find our calling without doing much work. I would say the opposite. Finding a calling is a stressful, hard thing, and it's OK for it to be that way. We think it's going to be this very delightful, 'unicorn moment.' That to me is not what a calling is. I think a calling takes a lot more effort."

Jon is pretty passionate about helping people do significant things with their lives. His most recent book is called, *Start: Punch Fear in the Face, Escape Average and Do Work that Matters.* In his book, Jon really encourages people to put in the effort needed for their calling. He doesn't have much patience for people who just say they want to do something for their calling, yet they're not doing anything about it. If a person told Jon that he wanted to be a writer and wasn't already writing, Jon would tell him, "No, you don't. You don't want to write, because writers write." So, in a nutshell, Jon's message is, "Get out there!"

"I think sometimes we want to find our calling without doing much work... We think it's going to be this very delightful, 'unicorn moment.' That to me is not what a calling is. I think a calling takes a lot more effort."

17

Step 7: Live Your Calling and Refine

Replace a smaller impact with a larger impact

Only one who devotes himself to a cause with his whole strength and soul can be a true master. For this reason mastery demands all of a person.

– Albert Einstein

When Rena and I first started our financial coaching business, we didn't know very much about how to market or even how to explain to people clearly what it was we did. It took a lot of practice, and there was a lot of trial and error. Eventually, we were able to tell people clearly what we did and how we could help them. We started out rough, but over time we refined our message.

We also refined our workshops. When we started out, we mostly shared our knowledge through teaching. Now in our workshops, attendees learn by experience rather than by just listening to us. We made a change when we noticed that attendees experienced only limited results when they simply sat back and listened to what we had to say.

The refining process is an important step in finding and living our calling. The main objective of this step is to maximize the effectiveness of our efforts.

Motives

Motives can get in the way and confuse us about what we are trying to accomplish. We may start to think that something's not working if we don't feel certain emotions. So we check our motives and remind ourselves about the results we initially set out to accomplish. Are we really trying to contribute to the world, or are we pursuing a certain feeling? Maybe deep down, we want recognition. Or perhaps we're trying to alleviate guilt.

It is natural for these types of motives to surface when we try to pursue our calling, but we need to be careful not to let them drive our efforts. Ultimately, our compassion for people is what we want driving us. We will have the maximum impact when our compassion aligns with our strengths.

It may seem a little odd that we are talking about motivation at the end of our steps, rather than at the beginning. We bring up this issue now because we have noticed that underlying motivations tend to pop up once we finally get into motion.

Perhaps we initially got into an endeavor for the right reasons, but once we get going, we discover we were secretly hoping to feel happy, to get some recognition, alleviate guilt, or have some other emotional benefit. Many of us won't even be aware that we have these hidden motivations until we're pretty far along in the journey. The key is to remain true to our original motives. Those desires can help us keep going.

A good way to keep the right motivation is to write down the results we want to achieve. When we have written down, for example, "People in poverty will transition to middle class," we can stay focused on those results. When we are tempted to give up in the face of opposition or setbacks, for example, we can refocus on the results. We can remind ourselves that we didn't get into this for the positive strokes, but to be a blessing to the people who are counting on us.

What Helps?

As we are in the process of refining our efforts, we need to take a close look at what helps people in the long run. Often we address the immediate visible or felt need. These needs are easy to spot and often straightforward to address. The folks we're influencing may even feel like we're helping them and be grateful. But the deeper needs continue.

An obvious example would be giving a drunk man money for a drink. The drunk may be appreciative, but we're not helping him. In fact, we might be harming him. A lot of helping in the world ends up enabling people to stay stuck. The poor stay poor. The homeless remain homeless. The uneducated drop out of school. We shift the burden of providing a solution onto ourselves, the intervener. But this encourages passive folks to continue letting others do for them what they need to do for themselves.

I'm not saying that we should withdraw all help and just let folks fend for themselves. We just need to be aware of the results in the bigger picture.

Some types of help can harm folks by creating an unequal relationship, with the helper doing all the work and the receiver just receiving. This gives a subtle message to the one being helped that they aren't capable and are dependent. Those being helped may even start to believe that they are insufficient – that they aren't capable of taking care of themselves.

Instead, we can set up a partnership with those in need: an equal relationship where we come alongside, adding creativity and resources to the solution. In this partnership, the ones in need are the initiator and creator of their own recovery[29]. With this approach, people being helped retain their dignity and their confidence.

We've seen firsthand that some things that appear to help don't help at all. We've given thousands of dollars to friends in need, and years later these friends are still living as they were. We've taken on clients who said they really needed our help, but couldn't afford our rates. So we gave them a deep discount or waived the fee completely. In the end, these clients rarely make significant change in their lives.

The truth is that we cannot change anyone. People can only change themselves. We can provide guidance, and we can partner with them. But lasting change needs to come from within the person.

Refining Our Contribution

We can contemplate different methods of helping that will be most effective, but just like in Step 6, sometimes we just won't know what's best until we try some things out. This principle will hold true as we seek to make our contribution to the world. We will teach classes, write blogs, mentor folks, donate money, or build a community, among other things.

Then we need to watch what happens. What is the depth of effective change? Do most people go back to old patterns, or do most people sustain a long-term change? Based on what we observe, we can make necessary adjustments to ensure the results we want.

An effective assessment requires the ability to observe the results we produce. Gathering this information can be tricky, but it is very important. We need to know that our efforts are producing the desired result. If, for example, one hundred thousand homeless folks come through a program we create, and 99% of them remain homeless, we're not being very effective.

In the pursuit of our calling, we need to plan on measuring the results in a tangible way. Examples can include surveys, questionnaires, interviews, or direct observation. It's important to have a plan to follow up with folks. For example, if we gave money to help a family adopt, did they adopt? If we are leading other leaders, have their leadership skills improved? Naturally, we can ask the leaders we worked with. Alternatively, we can ask people who interact with the leaders we worked with to learn about how their leadership has or hasn't improved.

Once we have measured results, we need to ask ourselves how we can improve our effectiveness. Maybe instead of classes, it would be more effective to mentor folks. Maybe we need to have better filters to determine whom we help, so we're helping the people who are really ready to change.

Focus on Results

We sometimes get so caught up in activity that it's easy to forget what we were initially hoping to accomplish. Sometimes we just launch into activity without even considering the results we hope to see. If an outsider were to look at the series of actions we've taken over the last few months, or maybe even years, there would be no discernible pattern at all – just randomness.

Consider, for example, a couple's household finances. The couple decides early on that they want to pay for their newborn, Johnny, to go to college. But as Johnny approaches college-age, we find that the couple has a nice home, two nice cars, some nice stereo equipment, a flat screen TV, and lots of iGadgets. There have been lots of visits to restaurants and numerous vacations. But there is no money saved for Johnny's college. The couple's activities didn't match up at all with their goal of sending their son to college.

We see a similar lack of focus in existing organizations, committees, and clubs. We often hear someone throw out the following question, "What do we want to do for the upcoming year?"

Then people give all sorts of answers. "Let's have a golf tournament." "I'd like a barbecue." "We should start a book club." "We should do service projects for the poor." "How about a fund raiser?" There is no direction guiding the suggestions. They are all over the map.

The opposite of this very common lack of focus is to lay down some clear goals, and align the activities to the goal. However, this mindset is called 'Results Oriented,' not 'Goal Oriented' for a reason. Too often we have a goal, so we plan an activity to achieve that goal. We may even accomplish the stated goal, but we don't always check that the results achieved the reason behind the goal. We leave the results up to fate.

Mindset 13: Results Oriented

Old thinking: "I plan for activities, and hope I see some results."

New thinking: "I plan for results, and tweak the activities until I get the results I want."

In order to be as effective as possible in our calling, we must be very clear on the results we are trying to achieve. It's easy to get caught up in doing "stuff" because those things seem like good ideas at the time. But the activities we do for our calling should be determined by the specific results we are working toward. After any activity, we should evaluate its results and modify any future activities until we get the results we want.

The following example shows the difference. Suppose that Bob and Sue want to build a sense of community in their neighborhood. Being goal oriented, Bob and Sue decide to host an event. Bob likes movies, so he votes to have a movie event. They survey the neighbors, pick out the best movie, pick the best time for everyone, and pop the popcorn. When the event begins, Bob, Sue, and all the guests are focused on the movie experience. Bob gets the movie going right away, turns off the lights in his home theater, and everyone watches the movie. When the movie is done, it's late, and everyone leaves.

Bob and Sue were goal oriented and they were proactive, but they didn't see the results they wanted. Because the focus was on the movie, there was little to no interaction between guests.

A Results Oriented mindset means that we stop focusing so much on the activity, and we focus on the results we want to see. Then we plan the activity, always checking to make sure the activity will produce the desired results. If the activity isn't producing the results we want within a reasonable amount of time, we don't throw up our arms and say, "Oh well, I guess that didn't work." Instead, we change the activity. And we keep changing the activity until we get the results we want.

If we extend the 'Bob and Sue' example, Bob and Sue learn that they had a fun activity, but it didn't do much in building a sense of community. So they try again. Bob still thinks that movies are a low key and non-intimidating way for new people to meet, so they try another movie night. But this time they keep their focus on the results. As they plan the second movie night, they plan for meet-and-greet time with light refreshments before the movie. They also plan to ask a few questions to the group to open up conversation if things seem a little slow. They also plan to evaluate the results after the event is over.

Any activity is just a method to accomplish the desired results. The activity should never be the main point. The results generated from the activity need to be our primary interest.

As we are living our calling, we need to keep our eye on the results. We are always in danger of falling into the trap of doing a lot of activity, which feels good, but having limited or no actual results. The best way to avoid this trap is to follow up with the people who are supposed to be benefiting from our efforts. For example, if I feel my calling is to mentor my employees, I should check up on these folks after a few years – even if they don't work for me any more. I want to know the long-term impact I've had on them. Do I need to make some adjustments to my approach?

Part of a Whole

A lot of times we have a short-sighted view of our place in the world. We have our "set of levers" that we can push or pull in life, and we focus on these few things. We've seen the problem frequently in big companies. Department A produces a product. Department B produces a very similar product. But Department A doesn't talk to Department B, so there are two products that have overlapping features that work in entirely different ways. As a result, there are many confused customers.

A book called *The Fifth Discipline*[30] explains this idea very well. In this book, the author describes an exercise called the Beer Game. I (John) have facilitated the Beer Game and the results always turn out the same.

The Beer Game is set up with two teams. The game simulates a retail distribution system for beer. There are two teams. Each team consists of three people, representing one of three positions: the brewery, the wholesaler, and the retailer. The game facilitator represents the customer.

In each round, transactions occur. The retailer sells to customers and places orders with the wholesaler. The wholesaler fills orders and places orders with the brewery. The brewery fills orders and determines production levels. When each player places orders, there is a delay of several rounds between the placement of the order and the fulfillment of the order. It also takes a few rounds for the brewery to produce beer.

The game plays for a few rounds with simple orders so everyone gets familiar with the game. Then the players are told that a new song has been played on the radio, and it has lyrics that talk about this specific brand of beer. As a result of the popular song, customers start buying more of this beer.

The retailer runs out of the beer and starts increasing orders to the wholesaler. But the retailer doesn't see his orders being filled right away. In the next round, the retailer fills some customer advance orders of the beer and is out of the beer before the round is up. The retailer places an even larger order for the beer. The next week it's even worse, running out of the beer even sooner. Just to be safe, the retailer quadruples his order.

> ## Mindset 14: Systems Thinking
>
> Old thinking: "I experience life as a series of disconnected events."
>
> New thinking: "Everything is connected, and I leverage my efforts by understanding key interactions."
>
> We are all part of larger systems, whether in business, education, family, organizations, community, or a myriad of other kinds of systems. Each part of a system affects different parts of the same system. We will have greater results in any change effort when we understand the interrelationships between the different parts of a system and how they affect each other.

The wholesaler's story is similar. The wholesaler starts seeing increased demand from the retailer, and begins to run out of stock. At each round, the wholesaler starts increasing orders, eventually placing a tenfold order by mid game.

Meanwhile the brewery struggles mightily to keep up with all the orders.

Finally, the backlog of orders starts to flow down the supply chain. The wholesaler eventually gets his tenfold order filled, but by this time, the orders from the retailer are zero. That's right, zero. The retailer now has more beer than they can use for several months. The wholesaler has warehoused enough beer for the next one hundred rounds, and the brewery is bankrupt because they can't sell any more of their oversupply of beer.

What really happened in the game was that the demand for the beer from the customers doubled when the song came out and held steady for the rest of the game. If we were to chart the actual demand compared to the orders, we wouldn't think we were charting the same events.

What the players are supposed to learn from this game is that we are part of a bigger system. We need to be aware of our place in the system to interact with and influence the whole system. Otherwise, the results can be very unexpected.

There are some key concepts to Systems Thinking. Understanding and applying these ideas can help us be more effective in our calling.

1.   **The System has feedback.**

    Systems have feedback. A simple system can have reinforcing feedback, or it can have balancing feedback.

    Reinforcing feedback is like a snowball effect. For example, good customer reviews of a product result in more people buying the product. If the product is good, this produces even more positive reviews, which then results in more customers.

    Balancing feedback works to achieve stability. For example, our bodies are set up to maintain an optimal temperature. If the temperature gets too hot, our bodies sweat to release heat. If it gets too cold, our bodies shiver to generate heat.

In the Beer Game, the retailer's orders affect the wholesaler's backlog. The size of the backlog affects how quickly the wholesaler can fill the retailer's orders. When the retailer's orders aren't being filled, the emotional response of the retailer is to place an even bigger order.

The Beer Game has balancing feedback loops between the players up the supply chain. When players place orders for more than the typical amount of beer, the system pushes back, creating backlogs.

2. **We often contribute to the problems we experience, even though we are unaware we're doing so.**

   In the Beer Game, each player played his or her position as if it was separate from the other positions. The players themselves caused the wild swings in orders and inventories of beer by the way they played.

   For example, the retailer kept increasing the size of the orders, depleting the inventory at the wholesaler. This caused the fulfillment of orders to take even longer.

3. **Our actions and their consequences are usually separated in time or location.**

   The effects of our actions often show up in other areas of the system. Even worse, there is usually a delay between our actions and the effects.

   For example, consider the process of getting the water temperature just right in the shower when there is a fifteen second delay between when we adjust the knob and when the water temperature changes. The longer the delay, the harder it is. We adjust the knob for hotter water. We don't feel it get hotter, so we adjust it more. Then we adjust it more. When the water finally reaches the temperature setting from the knob, it's scalding hot. So, we adjust it way down, probably making it too cold.

In the Beer Game, there was a delay of several rounds between placing orders and fulfillment of those orders. The retailer just sees that he doesn't have enough of the beer and orders more. He doesn't consider that orders made in the previous rounds are still on their way.

This delay makes it hard to respond to the system as it changes.

4. **There are usually non-obvious areas of high leverage that can produce really big results.**

Because of the different forms of feedback within the system, there are often many places within the system that we can adjust to produce results.

For example, when we provide discipline to our kids, we set up a balancing feedback loop. We watch our kid's behavior, and in response, we provide corrective input to our kid, which in turn, affects their behavior.

There are low leverage and high leverage ways to get our kids to behave well. The lowest leverage way to get our kids to behave is to punish the negative behavior. Because we don't instill in our child an internal motivation for good behavior, our kid only behaves well when there is an authority figure around. In this scenario, we are focusing all our energy on increasing the corrective input we provide to our kid.

A higher leverage approach would be to praise all the positive behaviors we see in our kid. This is what many animal trainers do for animals. These trainers don't punish bad behavior. They ignore these behaviors. Instead, they focus on reinforcing the positive behaviors they want to see in the animal. This approach works better than the punitive one above because over time our kid will want to exhibit the positive behaviors to get the praise or other reward. In this scenario, we initially focus our energy on the corrective input, but over time it takes less and less energy as our child behaves well on his or her own.

The highest leverage for the long term is to focus mainly on boosting the internal motivations of the kid for the good behavior. In this scenario, we aren't focused on specific behaviors, but on instilling a moral inventory in our child[31]. When our kid understands the reason why certain behaviors are wrong, counter-productive, or even self defeating, they will tend to do the right thing even in brand new situations they've never encountered before. In this scenario, we focus our efforts on the factors driving the kid's behavior, which is actually outside, but still connected to the discipline cycle we described above.

In the Beer Game, the highest leverage area in that system is with the retailer orders. If we can calm the retailer down, the whiplash effect throughout the rest of the system will be greatly reduced. This, of course, would be very non-intuitive to the player playing the brewery because the retailer player is the furthest down the chain.

5. **The system needs to be viewed as a whole.**

    As mentioned in *The Fifth Discipline*, dividing an elephant in half doesn't produce two small elephants. Unfortunately, breaking down the system into its components doesn't give us a better view of the system. Rather, it gives us an incomplete view of the system.

The players of the Beer Game view their role as separate from each other's roles. In their experience, players place beer orders with someone external to their part in the game.

If the players had viewed the whole system, they could have talked with everyone about the changing trends in the beer orders. The wholesaler and the brewery could have been more prepared for the increased orders.

Instead, the players probably had thoughts like, "What is this guy doing to me?" The other player's behavior seemed unexplainable and harmful.

There is a lot more about Systems Thinking than we can cover in this chapter. Mostly we want people to be aware of the systems in which they're operating. Systems don't just exist in product distribution. They are in our organizations. They exist in our internal thought and behavior processes. And they exist in society.

Whenever we experience limits to growth in our organization or in our own lives, whenever we see problems persist after great efforts to resolve them, whenever we miss or give up on our goals, there is likely a system in play.

When we use the Systems Thinking mindset in the pursuit of our calling, we will be more effective. We will influence and work with the system as a whole, rather than just an isolated part of it. We can learn to identify the high leverage areas within the system and increase our effectiveness.

Some Final Points to Consider

Also, we can use the Systems Thinking mindset to refine our contribution. To increase our effectiveness, we may not need to change what we're providing. We might just need to refine the systems of which we're a part, in order to be more streamlined and effective.

Perhaps, for example, there are other individuals or organizations that provide the same services or help the same types of folks we want to help. Instead of being in competition with them, we can talk to these organizations or individuals and find out how we can be more effective together. Perhaps we can both specialize in different areas and provide more focused effective help.

Maybe we've started a business. But in our desire to be successful, we must resist the temptation to be all things to all people. We can still work with other businesses that offer similar services to make sure we're meeting all the needs out there. Maybe we are coaching people to be leaders. Perhaps our competitor across town is doing the same thing. If we talk to them, maybe we'll find out that we really like coaching high school and college-aged folks, while our competitor loves to coach middle managers. Perfect. Now we can work with our competitor to produce better results and coach the target group of people we're happier coaching.

It's hard to fully describe how totally awesome it is to be living our calling. We are energized because we are using our strengths. We are excited because we are working on what we are passionate about. When we are mindful of the results of our efforts, we can know we are doing everything we can to maximize our life's impact. Then we will experience an incredible, deep sense of joy and satisfaction as we are truly having the time of our lives.

Key Points

- It's important for us to measure the effectiveness of our efforts to make sure we are getting the results we want.

- We want to make sure our help is benefiting and not actually inadvertently harming people, for example, by creating dependence.

- We are part of a bigger system. In order to be as effective as possible, we need to understand how the system affects us and also how we affect the system.

- We don't need to duplicate what is already being done. Instead, we can refine systems already in place to maximize effectiveness.

Exercises

1. If you have thoughts about your calling at this point, write down some key results you want to see.

2. Write down some possible methods that will help produce these results.

3. Write down some barriers that might get in the way of these results.

4. Write down some ways you can tangibly measure the key results you want to see.

18

Jenny Williamson

Founder and CEO, Courage Worldwide

It may be hard for an egg to turn into a bird: it would be a jolly sight harder for it to learn to fly while remaining an egg. We are like eggs at present. And you cannot go on indefinitely being just an ordinary, decent egg. We must be hatched or go bad.

– C. S. Lewis

For Jenny Williamson, life was perfect. She recalls, "My husband had an amazing job, and my kids were doing fabulous." Yet she longed for something more. As Jenny approached her 40th birthday, she started asking some tough questions. "Why am I on this planet? Is there more to life?" She says that although the questions weren't very original, they really tripped her up.

At the time, Jenny felt like she had no purpose, no calling and no talent. She says, "I absolutely couldn't figure out why I was taking up space on this planet except that my family loved me and needed me."

When Jenny asked God what she was supposed to be doing, she got a question back in return, "Do you have the courage to be you?" That response was confusing. She and God had the same conversation over and over. She asked what she should do and He asked who she would be.

Jenny says, "We wrestled that out for a long time, and God began to show me who He created me to be. He started to show me my childhood dreams." Jenny remembered that she'd wanted to be a missionary, travel the world and tell people about Jesus. She used to cry when she thought about people who didn't know Him.

Slowly, Jenny began to understand that those memories were clues to who she is and, therefore, what she should be doing. God was showing Jenny her heart in order to show her who He made her to be: an encourager, a water walker and a giant-slayer, to do things that had never been done before. It all started making sense to Jenny, because those dreams had been a big part of who she was as a child, but she had abandoned them over time. She shares, "I realized I had stopped being me along the way." Now God was asking her if she had the courage to be the person he made her to be.

Then God reminded Jenny how she had always wanted to have daughters. Jenny already had three sons. She recalls, "I couldn't figure out why He was bringing that up to me, because that felt like a dream that had died." At that point, God introduced the issue of child sex trafficking to her. She describes her conversation with God.

God: "Remember the daughters that you always wanted and longed for? Your daughters are being raped and tortured every day."

Jenny: "But I'm just a mom."

God: "Oh good, because that's exactly what they need."

Jenny felt called to rescue girls from the slavery of sex trafficking. She founded Courage to Be You (C2BU) to rescue girls and help them become the people God intended them to be. C2BU has blossomed into Courage Worldwide, and the organization is building Courage Homes not only in the U.S., but also around the world.

Jenny is an encourager at heart. She encourages people every day, whether she's addressing thousands of people from a stage, talking with a neighbor down the street or sitting with a girl at Courage House. She explains, "I'm always challenging and encouraging people to discover why they're on planet Earth and what their God-given identity is. I get to encourage new kids in their destiny, and I encourage them in their purpose." She says her passion is to teach people to be all that God has created them to be.

Jenny says her experience of life before and after finding her calling is as different as night and day. She tells people, "I spent the first 40 years of my life reacting to whatever would be thrown my way – financial circumstances, relational circumstance, any circumstance. It was just reactionary."

"Do you have the courage to be you, the 'you' God created you to be? That journey of discovering your identity is essential for your calling."

But now Jenny lives with purpose. Jenny explains that before time began, God imagined her and planned her, and now He has a special assignment for her. Jenny says, "I am so much more intentional about everything. I have lived more in the last ten years than I did in the first forty."

Jenny doesn't know if she will always be doing the same work she is doing today. She says that rescuing kids from sex trafficking and putting them in homes is the work God has on His calendar for her right now. She goes on to say, "Ten years from now, it could be homeless ministries. But I'm always going to be helping people find their identity and their destiny." The population she works with may change, but because she will still be Jenny, she will always be doing work that makes a difference in peoples lives.

According to Jenny, "When you find your calling, when you find your energy and your destiny, it does not mean that you do not have battles to fight. I guess this is probably the thing most people don't realize." Jenny recalls what it was like when she finally understood who she is and what she should be doing. She says, "All hell broke loose trying to stop me from becoming the person God created me to be, and doing all that I was created to do."

Right when Jenny was in the middle of finding her calling, she and her husband lost their home and moved to a new city where she didn't know anybody. God had placed an enormous dream on Jenny's heart to build homes for these girls, but she didn't have any experience doing fundraising, and she was living in a new place. She had to learn to rely on God to make the connections she needed to make her dream a reality.

There were other challenges, too. Her husband had cancer, and both of them were diagnosed with melanoma. Their kids were failing in school. Life went on. She says, "Every day there's something that comes up that tries to make me quit. I often tell people, 'winning just means you don't quit.' So I just vow everyday that I won't quit."

Now Jenny is learning about leadership. She wants to be prepared to be an effective leader during the crucial times that lay ahead. She shares, "I feel like God's preparing me as a leader to make this issue a more mainstream topic. Kids are talking a lot about it right now, but there are still a lot of people who really do not realize that our children are being hurt, even here in the United States."

As Jenny seeks to improve her own skills related to her calling, she has some advice for other people seeking to live their calling. She says, "I would ask them the same question that God asked me: Do you have the courage to be you, the 'you' God created you to be? That journey of discovering your identity is essential for your calling. Knowing your true identity is crucial to finding and fulfilling that goal."

19

The Character of the Called

Character is like a tree and reputation like a shadow. The shadow is what we think of it; the tree is the real thing.

– Abraham Lincoln

As Rena and I were starting our financial coaching business, we found that there was no shortage of advice on how to run our business. Often the people giving advice had something to sell. We got all kinds of comments like:

- "You have to have a brochure."
- "You have to advertise on Google adwords."
- "Don't advertise on Google. Advertise on Facebook."
- "You need to optimize your web site for search engine results."
- "You need a phone app."
- "You need to give to others first."
- "You need to speak to groups."
- "You must have business cards."
- "Name your company starting with the letter 'A'."
- "Don't advertise in the phone book. Nobody uses that anymore."
- "Advertise in the phone book. People still use it."

- "You've got to have a Facebook page."
- "Don't use Facebook for your business. Use Twitter instead."
- "You can't use an abstract company name like Zappos, Amazon, or Google, or your business will fail."

And on and on. While some of the advice was good, I (John) kept being reminded of a saying: "When you are a hammer, the world looks like a nail to you." (For example, when someone sells phone book advertising, every problem they see seems to be solvable by a phone book ad.)

We've learned two important lessons through this experience:

1. Each organization, business, and person is unique. What works for other organizations, businesses, or people may not work for you.

2. Everything flows from the person. Techniques, skills and methods don't work. What works is how the person shows up.

Everything Flows from the Person

The lesson that "Everything flows from the person" is key. Too often, we focus on what we are 'doing,' and we miss out on 'being', and being aware of who we are and what we bring to the situation. As we work on pursuing our calling, the most important asset we will provide is our own self.

Have you ever experienced something like this: Sally went to the cell phone kiosk, and the salesman tried to sell her one of their high-end phones. Sally could tell he was pretty slick, using all the right sales techniques. But Sally felt uncomfortable and told the guy, "No, thanks." Thirty minutes later, Sally was at a different kiosk on the other side of the mall. The salesperson there was really helpful, friendly, and genuine, and Sally bought the phone – the same phone the first salesperson tried to sell her. The second salesperson may have even used all the wrong sales techniques, but it still worked because the selling was from a different person – one that came across as more genuine and concerned about Sally's needs.

The truth is that techniques and skills don't work when a person is focused on him or herself. We can tell when the person just wants to make the sale and fill a quota. If the person has the right character and a good attitude, we can also tell, and we trust them. They may even lack skills or techniques, but we still trust the person. When we show up with the right stance, the skills and techniques can move us from good to great. This approach is also true when wooing people to join us in our calling.

Ongoing Effort

You may have noticed that developing character is not one of our steps. That's because character development is not a simple to-do item we can check off our list. It is a lifelong endeavor. We are challenged to live lives of integrity, every moment of every day.

I (John) have found that developing and building personal character can be very challenging. It's especially difficult to act with good character when it feels like an interruption, or when it will otherwise cost me. It is humbling to admit that on numerous occasions I have not acted with integrity or out of concern for other people.

One day, I was backing out of a tight spot in a parking lot. The lanes were narrow and the spaces were squeezed. I was watching all the sides and behind me, but I didn't turn tight enough to back into the narrow lane. Suddenly, I felt the car jolt. I had bumped into one of the cars across the lane.

I was in a real hurry, and I had to be somewhere in 30 minutes. So I jumped out, glanced at the car really fast, jumped back in, and took off. I looked only long enough to see if any damage was noticeable at a glance. To be honest, I don't really know if there was damage, because I didn't take the time to make sure. I didn't leave a note either.

In that moment, I didn't act with integrity. What I believed and what I valued didn't line up with my actions. I didn't act out of love and concern for the other car owner.

These types of situations will come up when we least expect them. Someone drops a hundred dollar bill. Do we pick it up and keep it? Do we tell the person? We have to decide in an instant.

Whether it's about integrity or other qualities we want to exhibit, we have to be constantly vigilant and intentional to show up with the qualities we value.

Essential Character Qualities

Character qualities aren't just about being a good citizen. These qualities are about how people experience us. Our success in our calling will be greatly influenced by the qualities we build into our character.

There are many qualities that will support us in our calling. Here we'll focus on three main character traits we believe have the deepest impact on our efforts and results. These traits are:

1. Integrity and Honesty
2. Love and Compassion
3. Boldness

Integrity and Honesty

To make a deep meaningful impact in people's lives, we need to hold ourselves to the highest levels of integrity. We should always strive to be honest with other people and ourselves. Like my earlier story demonstrates, it's really easy to have integrity only when it suits us.

Like I thought when I backed into the other car, in the moment, "Just this once, I'll take the convenient path." But the problem is that events aren't isolated, they are cumulative. As our choices in life are revealed, people learn whether or not they can trust us.

Wikipedia defines integrity as:

> A concept of consistency of action, values, methods, measures, principles, expectations, and outcomes.

People of integrity are consistent, showing themselves to be trustworthy in every area of their lives. Their actions agree with their principles. They do what they say. They are not hypocrites. When I look at this definition and think back on some of my own actions, I go, "Ouch!"

How trustworthy other people find us to be is a direct result of our levels of integrity and honesty. If people are going to work with us or interact with us, we will need to build trust with them. Otherwise, things will either move along at a snail's pace or stop at a standstill. When there is little trust, communication takes a lot longer, since we can't trust what each other is saying.

In my own experience, I've found that integrity is not something that just happens. I need to be intentional and work at it. Having integrity is a lot like peeling back the layers of an onion. As I acquire integrity in certain areas, I discover new areas that need work. There isn't anyone who shows 100% perfect integrity all the time. Everyone has some room for growth in this area. So, we encourage people to work on their integrity in specific areas, a few at a time.

Here is a simple way to make it easier to consistently live out your values. First, consider various situations where you are tempted to act opposite of your values. Then decide before you get into that situation what you are going to do. Consider the following example:

When I bumped that car in my earlier story, I had not carefully considered beforehand what my response would be if I was ever in a situation like that. Do I leave a note? Do I just leave? Do I pretend to do the right thing and then leave quickly? When I have to make a choice about my integrity right in the moment, there's a good chance I'll regret my choice later, because my feelings muddle up my brain. Making decisions ahead of time allows the opportunity to choose actions of integrity over emotional reactions.

Following is a list of some important areas where we will have frequent opportunities to live out our values. It may be worthwhile to consider in advance what values we will want to live out in these situations:

- In the way we drive our vehicles
- In our interactions with various people: kids, spouse, boss, family, friends, etc.
- In our workplace
- In following through on the commitments we make
- In our transactions and negotiations: purchases, bartering, and other agreements
- In our finances
- In our health
- In our spiritual life
- When we are by ourselves and no one is looking

Love and Compassion

The character qualities of love and compassion deal with our motivation. People can tell when we love them from a sincere place. People can also tell when we're wrongly motivated. Just like the example we cited earlier with the cell phone salesman, if we are focused only on ourselves, people get an uncomfortable feeling. It's a little spooky. Somehow, many people can just tell.

The key is to be sufficiently concerned for the other person and their needs and desires. When we interact with people with love and compassion, they will feel that we care for them. It sounds really simple, but in practice it's not so easy.

Often, our true motivations are clouded. For example, we may say we have compassion for the homeless. We want to have compassion for the homeless, but when we show up at the shelter, it's more about us and what *we're* doing. We feel noble for having helped at the homeless shelter, yet maybe we haven't really engaged with or reached out to the very people we are there to help.

I'm not proud to say that I've done this. I've participated in service projects where I called the people we were helping, "the Residents." I didn't treat them like real people. They were just objects of my service so I could go back home and pat myself on the back.

We can check our motivations from time to time by asking these important questions: "Am I seeing people as individuals with hopes, dreams, hurts, and fears? Or am I seeing them as objects – as an obstacle to overcome, a problem to be solved, an inconvenience to put up with, or a tool to accomplish a goal?"

When we find ourselves lacking love and compassion, the best way to change is to consider what a loving compassionate person would do. Consider what a good friend would do. Then do that. The reason this works is because our actions and our feelings aren't separate. Sometimes we feel, and then we act. Other times we act first, and then we feel.

Boldness

The character quality of boldness is about instigating change. If we are shy, avoiding risks, we are in danger of living someone else's calling rather than our own. In order to push through, we need to take some risks and bring about the change we envision.

Unfortunately we are not taught to be bold. Instead we are conditioned to be compliant. From the start of elementary school, we are taught to get in line, keep quiet, and do what we're told. This makes for great employees in the work place. However, this doesn't raise up people who initiate change in the world. This statement isn't a knock on teachers, principles, or other people who work in schools. This conditioning is just a result of the way our education system is set up.

Whatever calling we discover, we will encounter resistance. Even if we decide, for example, we want to be an awesome manager that brings out the best in our employees, we're going to encounter opposition. Opposition may come from other people in the company, or maybe even from our boss. But the worst resistance is the resistance that comes from within ourselves.

I know I've encountered a lot of internal resistance just writing this book. I've experienced fear of putting myself out there. I've also found myself suddenly more interested in just about anything other than writing this book as my subconscious tries to distract me from completing it. I had thoughts like, "What if people don't like what I have to say?" or worse, "What if people just ignore this book?" I've had to remind myself over and over that I am bold and compassionate. I can show my boldness and compassion by finishing.

Note that being bold doesn't mean we have to be obnoxious or disrespectful. Being bold just means that we initiate, we go first, we take risks, and we don't accept the status quo.

Boldness is like the character trait of integrity in that it also has many facets. There are often areas in our life where we are naturally bold, while there are other environments where we are naturally cautious.

We can practice boldness one area at a time, until we are naturally more bold than not. There may also be certain situations where we decide it's okay for us to not be so bold, which is fine as long as it's not the area of our calling.

Also, just as we discussed regarding the integrity quality, it's helpful to decide ahead of time how we're going to bring boldness to the situation. By making our decision in advance, we can avoid having to overcome discomfort and fear in the moment of the decision. For example, we may decide in that next department meeting, we're going to share a concern we have. (And if we are also showing the quality of love and compassion, we'll do this in a tactful, caring fashion.)

One way to practice being bold is to begin a habit of going first. If someone asks for a volunteer, decide in advance that you'll offer to do it without hesitation. If you're in a group setting, when it's time to share something, go ahead and share first. Going first is a form of boldness. You are taking a risk of looking foolish.

A part of boldness is also speaking up when we see something. Often we'll see someone go down a bad path, but we keep quiet because we don't want to offend him or her. But speaking up doesn't have to be offensive. We can choose the qualities of love and compassion when we speak and we'll find that we naturally use a style and manner that is not offensive.

The bottom line is, like the other character qualities, boldness doesn't just happen. For most of us, it requires effort. If boldness is a character quality you want to grow in yourself, pick some situations where you can be bolder and practice.

What's Next

In summary, as we pursue our calling, our interactions with other people will be influenced not only by our actions, but also by our way of being as well. Many people will be able to sense our motivations, our compassion, and our trustworthiness. Our calling is best supported when we first become the person we need to be, then having that "being-ness" flow into what we do.

If we want to develop our character, we start by identifying the qualities we want to focus on strengthening. Next, we look for opportunities to begin practicing those character qualities. We can decide in advance how we will handle certain situations, and we can take small steps to increase those qualities a little at a time.

Finally, it is helpful to continually remind ourselves of the qualities we are taking on. Affirmations are a great way to let these changes seep into our subconscious. For example, we can put up signs, and notes around the house and in the car. We can speak our qualities out loud when we wake up, when we're driving and when we go to bed. We can tell ourselves things like, "I am loving and compassionate", "I consistently act with honesty and integrity," and "I am bold."

As we continue to develop into our character the qualities of integrity, honesty, love, compassion, and boldness, the impact we can have on the world will be multiplied greatly.

20

Our Calling vs Our Kiddos:

Rock, Paper, Scissors?

If you raise your children to feel that they can accomplish any goal or task they decide upon, you will have succeeded as a parent and you will have given your children the greatest of all blessings.

– Brian Tracy

Perhaps up until now, you felt your calling was to be a parent. Now you're curious if there's more for you to pursue. Or maybe you're wondering how you could possibly find time to fit in a separate calling other than your role as parent.

We decided to address this topic in its own chapter, because we know that parenting is such a huge honor and responsibility. We also know firsthand that it is a huge challenge.

Fortunately, we don't have to pick one over the other, our calling or our kids. There's no need for "Rock, Paper, Scissors." We have found that when we pursue our calling and live the life we were born to live, our children ultimately win, too. Kids learn tools for success when they watch us discover and pursue our own calling. We can teach our kids to be thinking about and exploring their own calling on their life. Therefore, we think it is vital to involve our kids in our pursuit of a calling.

The Importance of the Role of "Parent"

The role of "parent" comes with the unique opportunity—and responsibility—to influence our children. Ultimately we want our kids to make their own meaningful contribution to society.

As we know from Steps 1 through 4, not having enough time, energy or money takes a heavy toll when raising kids. We sometimes end up parenting reactively instead of proactively. Sometimes it seems like damage control is the best we can hope for! Even though John and I (Rena) really value personal growth and do our best to be proactive in our parenting, there have been times when our biggest hope was to keep from passing on our own issues to our kids. In fact, we know a couple that jokes that they aren't saving for their kids' college. Instead, they are saving for the therapy their kids will need to undo the damage they as parents are causing!

Seriously though, it's important for us to recognize that the impact we have on our kids will likely run deeper than the impact we have on any other person. Similarly, the effect we have on their lives likely will be deeper than the effect any other person has on them. It is important to be intentional about parenting, because the effects are so far-reaching. Like sowing seeds that produce a large crop, our children will go on to impact others. This impact will be affected by the choices we make as parents. Naturally, we want that influence to be a good and fruitful one.

Proactive Parenting

As parents, we must decide in advance what lessons we want our children to learn and deliberately create opportunities to teach them those lessons. We can't wait around for the right opportunity to present itself. We can't assume that schoolteachers, or even church youth group leaders, will instill the values we want our kids to have. Instilling values is our job as parents. There are some things our kids need to learn specifically from us rather than from someone else.

Here are some questions to help us start thinking about what we want for our own family:

- What is our vision for our family?
- What is our family's identity?
- What is important to our family?
- What characteristics do we value?
- What specific qualities do we want to instill in our children?
- How do we want to shape and mold the character of our children, including, for example, honesty, integrity, work ethic, and the value of relationships?

Our kids are always watching us and learning from us (even when we don't really want them to). It's like the saying goes, "Your actions speak so loud, I can't hear what you're saying." We want to be mindful about what our kids see us do, as well as what we say.

Of course, there are no perfect parents, no matter how hard we try. We've found that it is helpful for us to share with our kids what we are learning, how we are growing, where we sometimes struggle, and what our goals are. So, as we've learned about managing our money, our kids learned about managing money. As we've learned about significance and a calling, our kids have been learning, too.

Bring the Kids Along on the Journey

We have a great opportunity to raise our kids to discover their calling as they mature and develop. This is their time to explore. As parents, we should encourage them to try lots of different things and have a variety of experiences.

We can directly involve them in the activities we explore for our own calling. They will watch us and learn from us, even as we ourselves are learning. They will have a front row seat, seeing what it means to make a difference in the lives of other people. Watching us live out our values will speak louder than any lesson they will ever read in a book.

Our children should always benefit from our calling. Because of the demands and responsibilities of raising children, our calling is first to our kids and then to others. Our parenting should fit in with our calling. If it does not, what we've identified as our calling may be too specific and, therefore, too limiting.

I (Rena) shared my own story a little as part of Step 5. Let's revisit that story briefly so I can explain what I mean.

My Experience

Years ago, John read a book about personal mission statements and was working on crafting his own. He encouraged me to come up with my own mission statement as well. I was quite clear in my own mind—my goal was to "raise our boys to be Godly men." John didn't think that was a good mission statement. It didn't address what I would do when they were grown. Frankly, I didn't care. I knew what I wanted to accomplish, and that was good enough for me.

Years later, I did the work outlined in Step 5 and crafted my personal purpose statement. It was short and succinct. It stated simply, "I inspire meaningful proactivity." That little phrase might not seem like much to anyone else. But that's okay, because it's for my benefit. For me, each word is dripping with meaning. Another less elegant way of stating my purpose is that I get people moving to do important stuff. That's what I do.

I found that when I finally identified my purpose, it easily folded in with my goals as a parent. I definitely work to inspire meaningful proactivity in my kids, too. Sometimes my work with them has to take precedence over my work with other people. My responsibility is first to raise them well and then to benefit other people. These two things are by no means mutually exclusive. In fact, I think my kids benefit greatly from seeing the work John and I do with other people.

The main difference in what I called my mission statement, and what I now have as my personal purpose statement is this: originally, my focus was solely on my kids. Now my focus has expanded beyond my kids, but still includes them at the core of it. I can live my calling, be a mom, and still bless other people at the same time.

Harmony

Harmony between our family and our calling is the key. Some parents may be inclined to be out of harmony like I was in the past, giving up on the opportunity to influence other people and focusing only on parental responsibilities. Other parents may be out of harmony in the opposite way by not including their family in the work of their calling.

The last thing John and I would want is for people to hear our message, go out into the world to follow their calling, and forget to give their family the time, effort and attention it needs and deserves. As parents, we need to invest ourselves into our kids and raise them so that they, too, will be great influencers and blessings to many people.

In summary, a calling includes, but is not limited to, parenting. While a calling always goes beyond a single role, it cannot neglect the very important role of "parent."

21

The Question I Didn't Ask

Our lives begin to end the day we become silent about things that matter.

– Martin Luther King, Jr.

During my heart attack, there was an essential question that I (John) didn't ask. While I didn't ask this question of myself, I believe it's a question that most people will ask. The question I'm talking about is, "What will happen to me after I die?"

We contemplate this question throughout our life, but often it's asked in the realm of theory or philosophy. When facing the end of our life, theory and philosophy don't matter any more, and this question becomes much more personal. We want to know what's going to happen to us, right now.

This question can lead to a whole host of other questions such as, "Is there a God?" and "What is His attitude towards me?" Maybe we will wish that we had paid more attention in Sunday school all those years back!

The reason I didn't need to ask this question during my heart attack is because I already had an answer for what would happen to me after I died. This question was already settled for me in my mind and heart.

If you don't have an answer for this question, I encourage you now to spend time searching. If you find yourself lying awake at night, wondering about where you might end up after you die, it's probably worth a few lost hours of sleep. If you are still unsure about the answer, my hope would be that you put your calling on hold until you have a clear answer. I believe it's that important.

If you will bear with me for a bit, I'd like to introduce you to my friend, Jesus. The Jesus that I know is very different from the Jesus that a lot of people talk about or the one we see in the media. I think there is a lot of confusion in the world about Jesus and Christianity, and I'd like to share with you about a Jesus that gets lost in the noise. It is up to you to decide to accept this or discard what you read, but I'd like to have the opportunity to share the Jesus I've come to know.

Good or Bad

The idea that many people have about Christianity is that if you're a bad person, you are going to be sent to hell. It's as if God is waiting to pounce on us the moment we make a wrong choice. There are all kinds of misconceptions about Jesus, God, and Christianity. I've heard a lot of different things from people, both those claiming to follow Christ and those who don't. Perhaps you have heard some of these things as well:

1. I will make it into heaven if I avoid doing anything bad.
2. If my good deeds outweigh my bad deeds, I'll make it into heaven.
3. There's no heaven or hell. Christianity is just a control mechanism to elicit good behavior from people.
4. If I mess up, God will be mad at me, and bad things will happen in my life.

5. All those Christians are hypocrites. They tell me to do one
    thing, yet they do another.

Ideas about faith, religion and God have become twisted up. We treat
God like he's the IRS. If I just fill out this "form" the right way, I'm
in - as if Jesus is a dispassionate judge, jury and executioner. The
problem is that none of these viewpoints represent the Jesus that I
know. I hardly think that Jesus came down from heaven to die on a
cross just to keep us in line.

If we use the courtroom analogy for the way God works, Jesus is not
the judge or the jury. Instead, He is our defense lawyer. If we don't
have a defense lawyer in this court, we are in big trouble. The truth
is, doing good deeds doesn't wipe out the bad we've committed first
in our hearts and in our actions.

In an earthly courtroom, if we've stolen a car, the fact that we gave to
a charity doesn't enter into the debate. Our good deeds don't erase,
or counterbalance, the law that we've broken.

So, what can we say to defend ourselves in this heavenly court? The
answer is that there's nothing we can say. We've murdered people in
our hearts. We've committed adultery in our hearts. We've
misrepresented the truth. We've kept silent when the right thing
would have been to speak up. And this is just getting started. The
only thing we can do is to have the defense lawyer, Jesus, on our side.

And what can Jesus do that we can't? Well, if we've accepted Jesus'
gift of forgiveness, He doesn't just plead for mercy and grace for us.
No, He demands justice on our behalf. You see, if we accept Jesus'
offer of forgiveness, He has already paid for our wrongs. And it
would be unjust to have to pay twice for the same sins. This is the
only defense that works[32].

Jesus wants to be our defense lawyer in this heavenly courtroom. He
is not mad at us. He is not indifferent to us. When we accept Jesus as

our defense lawyer, we can take our focus off of avoiding sin and focus on loving people more and more.

To put it bluntly, we are not saved by anything we do or don't do. Either we are judged by our actions, which would not be good, or it all lands on Jesus. Followers of Jesus shouldn't be characterized by rules they follow or fail to follow. Rather, Christ followers should be characterized by love, and it aggravates me to see the opposite presented so often.

The God Who Wastes

If God was motivated only by justice, as people often believe, He wouldn't have sent Jesus to die on the cross. The cross doesn't help God give out justice any better. God sent Jesus to die on the cross because He is motivated primarily by love.

A friend of ours who is a minister, Troy Dean, has a great way to explain the nature of this love. It starts with a parable that Jesus told:

> "There was a man who had two sons. The younger son spoke to his father. He said, 'Father, give me my share of the family property.' So the father divided his property between his two sons.

> "Not long after that, the younger son packed up all he had. Then he left for a country far away. There he wasted his money on wild living. He spent everything he had.

> "Then the whole country ran low on food. So the son didn't have what he needed. He went to work for someone who lived in that country, who sent him to the fields to feed the pigs. The son wanted to fill his stomach with the food the pigs were eating. But no one gave him anything.

*"Then he began to think clearly again. He said, 'How
many of my father's hired workers have more than
enough food! But here I am dying from hunger! I will
get up and go back to my father. I will say to him,
"Father, I have sinned against heaven. And I have
sinned against you. I am no longer fit to be called your
son. Make me like one of your hired workers."' So he
got up and went to his father.*

*"While the son was still a long way off, his father saw
him. He was filled with tender love for his son. He ran
to him. He threw his arms around him and kissed him.*

*"The son said to him, 'Father, I have sinned against
heaven and against you. I am no longer fit to be called
your son.'*

*"But the father said to his servants, 'Quick! Bring the
best robe and put it on him. Put a ring on his finger
and sandals on his feet. Bring the fattest calf and kill it.
Let's have a big dinner and celebrate. This son of mine
was dead. And now he is alive again. He was lost. And
now he is found.'*

"So they began to celebrate."[33]

The first thing to understand is how presumptuous this son is. He
basically told his father, "Dad, I'm tired of waiting around for you to
die. I want my inheritance now." That's pretty rude, but the father
does it anyway. The father sells half of his estate so he can give it to
his son.

If this were a real life situation, this request wouldn't have been the
first time the son had been so rude and disrespectful to his dad. It

would have come after a long series of belligerent behaviors. So, the son takes the money and heads out, not to find himself or to find his place in life. Instead he goes off to indulge in some wild living.

This parable has been told and talked about by many people. Usually people focus on the son who leaves and comes back, but let's instead look at the father in this story. The parable reads, "While the son was still a long way off, his father saw him." When you read this story, you don't get the impression that the father just happened to notice his son coming. Instead, it would seem that the father must have been looking for his son to return.

The father must have stood out at the edge of his ranch looking for his son every day. His son was always on his mind. If he visited with his neighbors, I'm sure the topic would have come up. And the neighbors probably would have said, "You're wasting your time. That kid is never coming back. You know your son doesn't care about you. He just saw you as a bank account. You're worrying yourself to death. The best thing for you would be to just forget about the kid and move on with your life." But the father continued to go out every day, wearing out the horizon with his eyes, looking for his son.

The father "wasted" his time thinking about his son. He wasted his thoughts, and he didn't move on with his life. He wasted his life hoping to see his son again.

Most people would agree that the father in this parable represents God. He is the same way with us. In fact, it's even more profound. It's generally believed that God, who exists outside of time, knows what we will choose in our life – even before we make that choice. God knows who will choose Him and who will reject Him. But God doesn't just focus all His energies on those He knows will accept Him. Instead, God continues to pursue those He knows will ultimately reject Him.

God, too, wastes His energy and His efforts pursuing people. God knows who will reject Him, and yet He pursues these people anyway. God is wearing out the horizon with His eyes looking for you to come home.

Now that's an unfathomable love.

Father

The God of Christianity is not the "boogey man out to get you." God is not like Santa Claus, keeping a record of rights and wrongs. God doesn't weigh your good deeds against your bad ones to see if you've been good enough to make it in to Heaven. God isn't like a dispassionate policeman in the sky, making sure you follow the rules.

Instead, God is like a father motivated by love. Jesus even says that we should refer to God affectionately, like children calling their father "Daddy."

I learned more about God when I became a father to my kids. I have two boys. They are a lot of fun, and they are a lot of work. I am not their friend. I am not their boss. I am not their policeman. I am not their mentor. Though, there is a bit of each of these in my relationship with my kids. I am their father.

If my kids came to me and said, "Father, I have washed the bathroom. I have cleaned the toilets. I have made my bed and cleaned my room. I have fed the cats. Now, do you love me?" I would think something is seriously wrong with my kids – or with me.

My love for my kids doesn't depend on what they do or don't do. I love my kids because they are my kids. And if my kids thought that my love was dependent on their chore list, there would be a serious communication breakdown.

Both my kids and I would be missing out on a great father-child relationship. We would miss out on the fun we can have together.

My kids would miss out on teaching moments, and all the other great experiences and lessons we can have in a proper parent-child relationship. I would be really sad if my kids thought the chore list defined our relationship.

I believe that God wants a similar parent-child relationship with us. He wants us to know Him, not just do stuff for Him. As my pastor, Chuck Wysong, says, "God doesn't want a religion with you. He wants a relationship with you."

Choice

Some of you reading this may have a hard time believing that God even exists. A lot of scientific evidence seems to point to there not being a God. There is also a lot of scientific evidence that points to the existence of God.

But if God was just out there for everyone to see, if there was no doubt about the existence of God, and if God was in your face, what could you choose? Many people would feel coerced into choosing God.

There is even an Aesop fable about this. An unmarried king notices a young woman in a village. She isn't royalty, but he wants to pursue her anyway. Now, if he were to just walk into her village with his entourage and ask her to come to his court, what could she say? He is the king. The king would never know if the woman picked him because she wanted to, or if she just said, "Yes," because he was the king.

So, he disguises himself as a peasant and lives in her village for a while to see if he can woo her. As the story goes, he wins her over and finally reveals who he is.

In the same way, God isn't in our face. If you want to find evidence that God doesn't exist, you will find it. If you want to find evidence that God does exist, you will find it.

Ultimately the choice is yours. Right now, I passionately encourage you to seek your own answers. This is too important to let someone else decide for you. Don't just accept someone else's opinion. Investigate the answers on your own.

Read books – not just ones you already agree with. Then check on their references. Don't discount the content by saying the author is biased. All authors are biased. There are no objective perspectives on God and eternity. Test the truth of what these authors say. Do they make sound arguments? If you're not sure where to start, you might check out some of the books by the following authors: Lee Strobel, Josh McDowell, and William Lane Craig.

Honestly, you don't want to face the end of your life, and suddenly have this unanswered question about God and eternity.

22

Touch Lives

A life is not important except in the impact it has on other lives.

– Jackie Robinson

We want to wrap up by sharing some pointers to help stay on track based on our experience of finding our calling:

1. Surround yourself with like-minded people.

2. Never stop learning and stretching yourself.

3. Stay motivated by love.

4. Never give up!

Surround Yourself with Like Minded People

As we mentioned in Step 2 about connecting to positive inputs, it is very important to find some people who also want to live their legacy. These people will not be stuck in conventional wisdom. They will also be looking to make their splash in the world.

These folks will understand why we're out on the weekends learning public speaking or hanging out at local non-profit organizations.

These folks will empathize with our struggles, and they will push us to keep going.

It will be worthwhile to seek these people out. We can often find them in business settings, at local meet-up groups, and in our local non-profit organizations.

Never Stop Learning and Stretching Yourself

To keep increasing our influence and impact on the world, we can't just get to a good place and stop. We need to always be learning and growing. As we learn and stretch ourselves, we can increase the depth of the positive changes we are creating in the world.

Every once in a while, we should look up and ask ourselves, "When was the last time I tried something for the first time?" If it's been a while, maybe it's time to do something stretchy.

Stay Motivated by Love

Often times, we can get all twisted up in our motivations. If the calling we're pursuing also brings in cash flow, it can be tempting to make it about the money. Or our calling may make it easy to focus more on the fame and reputation.

We just need to stay connected to our motivation of love. If we show up *without* love, people will sense it. If we show up *with* love, people will sense it. Always remember that the reason for discovering your purpose and calling, making a splash in the world, and living a legacy at its core, is love.

Never Give Up

In life, there are times when we get tired and burnt out. We hit obstacles. Our plans flop. We may be tempted to give up and go back to our old way of living. We want to encourage you to keep going.

Regardless of how discouraged you might get at some point, you still have a unique contribution to give to the world. No one else can specifically do what you do. The world wants you to be your unique self and contribute. The world needs you and is waiting for you.

Keep in mind that living your legacy might look different than you originally thought it would, and that's okay.

So when you are dog tired or burned out, rest up, regroup, reconnect and recommit to your purpose, and make another go at it.

Send off

The conventional wisdom out there is to work 9 to 5, work to increase one's life style, and squeeze as much fun and enjoyment out of life as possible. In our experience, following this conventional wisdom leads to a life that is neither fulfilling nor satisfying. In particular, it doesn't help us answer the two questions that John asked during his heart attack:

"Did I love people well? "

"Did my life matter? "

Our hearts desire for you is that you will choose the best path that life has to offer you. We wish for you to live in such a way as to have amazing answers to these two questions. The water is fine. Go make a splash!

Go to http://www.simplygreatlives.com to get connected, stay motivated, and let us know how you're doing. We can't wait to see the splash you make in the world with your life!

Appendix A

Mindsets to Help You Live Your Calling

Mindsets are beliefs about how the world works. They shape our expectations of ourselves and of other people. They tell us what is possible and what is not. Our mindsets will either hold us back or propel us forward. Following are the mindsets we have found to be critical to living our calling.

Mindset 1: Empowerment Mentality

Located in Step 1: Make Time

Old thinking: "I have to.../I can't..."

New thinking: "I choose to..."

When we don't take responsibility for the choices we make, we forfeit the power to choose something different for ourselves. Therefore, there is a lot of power in recognizing our part in what we might otherwise consider to be our "circumstances." We need to recognize our own power to make changes in our lives before we will have the power to affect changes in the lives of other people.

Mindset 2: Abundant Options

Located in Step 1: Make Time

Old thinking: "I have two options, A or B."

New thinking: "I have many options."

We are fooling ourselves when we believe there are only two choices or, worse, when we believe there are no choices at all. A or B thinking is just a different version of victim mentality. We will have more power over our own lives when we search for a variety of options before we make our decision. The truth is there is an abundance of options available. Brainstorming solutions will reveal new options, usually with at least one of them being better than the first two we started with.

Mindset 3: Outward Focus

Located in Step 2: Connect to Positive Inputs

Old Thinking: "I need to be happy before I help others."

New Thinking: "I will find ultimate satisfaction when I am other-focused."

We experience a shallow, fleeting happiness when we focus just on ourselves, doing things like traveling and buying nice stuff. When we do things that benefit other people, we experience a deeper, longer-lasting satisfaction. The key is to not wait until we're "feeling satisfied" with our own life because that satisfaction isn't going to come until we have that outward focus.

Mindset 4: Continuous Learning

Located in Step 2: Connect to Positive Inputs

Old Thinking: "I'm done with school, so I'm done learning."

New Thinking: "I'm a lifelong learner."

Living our calling will require us to learn many new things like new ways of thinking, new ways of expressing ourselves, and new ways of doing things to name a few. It takes some humility to admit that we don't know it all, but no one person really can know everything. Having a continuous learning mindset will allow us to always improve our effectiveness in our calling.

Mindset 5: Openness

Located in Step 3: Maximize Your Energy

Old thinking: "I can't trust new ideas or new opportunities."

New thinking: "I am discerning and let good things into my life."

We must be willing to consider new ideas in order to grow. At first, being open to new ways of thinking can be a little scary. This openness does not have to threaten our closely held personal beliefs, though. We always have the power to accept, reject or modify new ideas to make them work for us. Being open to new perspectives, ideas, and ways of doing things helps us greatly in being effective in our calling.

Mindset 6: Win-Win Or No Deal

Located in Step 3: Maximize Your Energy

Old thinking: "I want a solution that's good for me."

New thinking: "A solution is only acceptable if it's good for everyone involved."

We know there are many potential solutions to any given problem. When negotiating, therefore, we might as well assume there is a solution that will benefit both us and the other people involved. Opting for win-win solutions helps foster trust because people like knowing that we have their best interests at heart.

Mindset 7: Financial Freedom

Located in Step 4: Build Security at Home

Old Thinking: "I need to use credit to achieve my goals."

New Thinking: "Being debt free gives me more freedom and opportunities."

Personal money management will affect our calling. When we have money set aside for emergencies and no debt, we are in a relatively secure position financially, compared to a person who has debt and no cash. Having this kind of security keeps us from getting stuck in a bad situation, like needing to stay in a job we don't like because we need the money. It also opens up many more options for how we choose to live our calling than we would have otherwise.

Mindset 8: Risk Management

Located in Step 4: Build Security at Home

Old Thinking: "I value safety over risk."

New Thinking: "I take appropriate risks in life."

It is tempting to play it safe in life. But if we are to do worthwhile things in the lives of other people, we must be willing to take some risks. Some risks will be personal, like trying new things, looking silly to other people, and maybe even failing at a new venture. Other risks may involve our career, our relationships, or our finances. We will be more able to tolerate these risks when we know our needs will be met and we feel reasonably secure physically, emotionally, and financially.

Mindset 9: Unbalanced

Located in Step 5: Discover Your Purpose

Old thinking: "I need to improve my areas of weakness."

New thinking: "I maximize my strengths."

We will achieve the best results in our calling when we focus on and utilize our strengths. We will get very limited results by trying to shore up our weaknesses. Therefore let's just work to bring our weaknesses up to a minimum acceptable level when they are holding us back. Then we can focus on using our strengths for the benefit of other people. Working in our areas of strength yields extraordinary results, not to mention lots of personal satisfaction and joy.

Mindset 10: Calling Mentality

Located in Step 5: Discover Your Purpose

Old thinking: "I just need to serve somewhere."

New thinking: "I use my strengths and passions to serve effectively."

Many of us have helped out various charities, but our efforts may have been unfocused and, therefore, the results we got may have been very limited. A calling, determined by our unique combination of strengths and passions, is much more focused than doing some volunteer work here and there. This focus is one of the main reasons living our calling is far more effective at bringing about long-lasting change in the lives of other people.

Mindset 11: Agile Planning

Located in Step 6: Learn by Experience

Old thinking: "I make the whole plan and then follow it."

New thinking: "The plan isn't fully knowable until I take steps forward."

Even though it's uncomfortable not fully knowing what to expect, we must be willing to set out on this journey without knowing all the details in advance. We will begin a cycle of doing, learning and re-planning. This agility allows us to take the steps we can do now, and from there, plan the next steps based on what we've learned along the way.

Mindset 12: Embrace Failure

Located in Step 6: Learn by Experience

Old thinking: "Failure is bad. Avoid it at all costs."

New thinking: "Failure is valuable because we learn from our mistakes."

It is normal to not get it right the first time we try something new. Many of us will avoid trying something new if there's a good chance we'll fail. When we are willing to venture out into the realm of new experiences, we will learn at a much faster pace than when we are playing it safe. In fact, failure gives valuable experience that helps us grow, experience we could never learn from a book. We will need to learn new concepts, try new things, and acquire new skills to live our calling. Therefore, we should not only expect to experience some failure during our journey, we might as well embrace it.

Mindset 13: Results Oriented

Located in Step 7: Live Your Calling and Refine

Old thinking: "I plan for activities, and hope I see some results."

New thinking: "I plan for results, and tweak the activities until I get the results I want."

In order to be as effective as possible in our calling, we must be very clear on the results we are trying to achieve. It's easy to get caught up in doing "stuff" because those things seem like good ideas at the time. But the activities we do for our calling should be determined by the specific results we are working toward. After any activity, we should evaluate its results and modify any future activities until we get the results we want.

Mindset 14: Systems Thinking

Located in Step 7: Live Your Calling and Refine

Old thinking: "I experience life as a series of disconnected events."

New thinking: "Everything is connected, and I leverage my efforts by understanding key interactions."

We are all part of larger systems, whether in business, education, family, organizations, community, or a myriad of other kinds of systems. Each part of a system affects different parts of the same system. We will have greater results in any change effort when we understand the interrelationships between the different parts of a system and how they affect each other.

References

1. The Chronicle of Philanthropy, cited on christopherreeve.org
2. http://www.courageworldwide.org
3. http://www.ihaveadreamfoundation.org
4. Collins, Jim Good to Great (HarperCollins, New York 2001)
5. http://michaelhyatt.com/videos/an-interview-with-john-c-maxwell-about-personal-development
6. http://www.nielsen.com/us/en/newswire/2012/the-cross-platform-report-a-new-connected-community.html
7.

    http://www.emarketer.com/newsroom/index.php/consumers-spending-time-mobile-growth-time-online-slows/
8. http://www.nielsen.com/us/en/newswire/2010/social-media-accounts-for-22-percent-of-time-online.html
9. Thornburg, Kristopher M.. "The effect of positive and negative messages on problem solving in computer programming tasks." PhD diss., University of Iowa, 2010.

10. Monkey & banana study: Stephenson, G. R. (1967). Cultural acquisition of a specific learned response among rhesus monkeys. In: Starek, D., Schneider, R., and Kuhn, H. J. (eds.), Progress in Primatology, Stuttgart: Fischer, pp. 279-288.

11. Cloud, Dr. Henry and John Townsend Boundaries: When to Say Yes, How to Say No to Take Control of Your Life (Zondervan, Grand Rapids, Michigan 1992)

12. Leonard, George Mastery (Plune a division of Penguin Books, New York, NY 1992)

13. Stanley PhD, Thomas J The Millionaire Next Door: The Surprising Secrets of America's Wealthy (Pocket Books, New York, NY 1996)

14. Brony Study (http://www.bronystudy.com/)

15. Idleman, Kyle, "Not a Fan: A Follower's Story" DVD (Not a Fan studio, 2011)

16. Fredrickson, Kim Building a Compassionate Relationship with Yourself (Kim Fredrickson, Roseville 2013)

17. Philippians 4:8, The Bible (New International Version)

18. Cloud, Dr. Henry and John Townsend Boundaries: When to Say Yes, How to Say No to Take Control of Your Life (Zondervan, Grand Rapids, Michigan 1992)

19. Fisher, Roger, William L. Ury, and Bruce Patton Getting to Yes: Negotiating Agreement Without Giving In (Penguin Books, New York, NY 1991)

20. Covey, Stephen The 7 Habits of Highly Effective People (Simon and Schuster, New York, NY 1989)

21. Heath, Chip and Dan Heath , Switch: How to Change Things When Change is Hard (Broadway Books, New York 2010)

22. Ramsey, Dave The Total Money Makeover (Thomas

Nelson, Inc, Nashville, TN 2007)

23. http://www.gallupstrengthscenter.com

24. Rath, Tom Strenths Finder 2.0 (Gallup Press, New York, NY 2007)

25. Buckingham, Marcus and Donald O. Clifton Now, Discover Your Strengths (The Free Press, New York, NY 2001)

26. Kawasaki, Guy The Art of the Start: The Time-Tested, Battle-Hardened Guide for Anyone Starting Anything (Portfolio, New York, NY 2004)

27. Dungy, Tony and Nathan Whitaker Uncommon: Finding Your Path to Significance (Tyndale Momentum, Carol Stream, IL 2011)

28. http://www.coachdungy.com/index.php/the-one-year-uncommon-life-daily-challenge/take-the-uncommon-life-challenge/

29. Twist, Lynne The Soul of Money: Reclaiming the Wealth of Our Inner Resources (W. W. Norton & Company, New York, NY 2003)

30. Senge, Peter The Fifth Discipline: The Art & Practice of The Learning Organization (Doubleday, New York, NY 2006)

31. Ezzo, Gary and Anne Marie Ezzo Growing Kids God's Way: Biblical Ethics for Parenting (Workbook) (Growing Families International, Simi Valley, CA 2000)

32. Talk: "The Addict, the Accuser, and the Advocate", Zack VanDyke (http://zachvandyke.com)

33. Luke 15:11-24, The Bible (New International Reader's Version)

Acknowledgements

We are thrilled to present this book to the world and trust that it will benefit many people. We would not have been able to produce this book without the help of some awesome individuals.

We are super-grateful to Brian Sharp. He helped us recognize that in our hearts, we needed to help people live their calling. He guided us through the transition from Steam Engine Financial Coaching to Simply Great Lives. Thanks, Brian!

Several people read our book's second draft, which was, shall we say, rather rough. They gave us feedback that was more valuable than we can express. Many thanks to Kathy Fairbanks, Bob Lusk, Brian Sharp, Jennifer Peterson, and Janet Wolke. Your feedback was crucial to making this a book people will enjoy reading.

We give special thanks to the participants of our first webinar series walking through our seven steps. The experience was kind of bumpy and they didn't even have a book to read. Their feedback helped us refine the content of this book. To Samantha Covington, Kathy Fairbanks, Barbara Frost, and Wolfgang Reißnegger: Thanks a ton to each of you for hanging in there with us!

We are thankful for Josh Loyst who created an awesome design for the book cover. We really appreciate your patience in working with us, Josh.

We want to recognize, give lots of thanks to and, well actually, boast about our editor Barbara Frost. She was fantastic to work with! She had great feedback that dramatically improved the book's readability. The work she did ended up being "heavy editing," which we think is a technical term that means it took her a lot of work to make our stuff this good. We are super-grateful, Barbara!

Finally, we are grateful to God who really makes everything possible.

Index

Made in the USA
Middletown, DE
22 June 2015